## Advance Praise for *Open Doors, Open Hearts*

This little book immediately transported me. . . . Rachel Kamin has collected and set like jewels in a splendid necklace over two dozen assorted real-life episodes of ordinary Midwestern American Christians set loose in China to experience the power that Jesus Christ has to open doors and open hearts. The vignettes are deceptive in their simplicity, yet awesome in their spiritual power. And inspirational! Real mission work is happening today when our children and grandchildren leave their cozy and nurturing American church homes and venture East.

*Dr. John C. Lawrenz*
*Former president of Asia Lutheran Seminary*

*Open Doors, Open Hearts* shares the stories of beautiful Chinese souls coming to Christ through their encounters with American teachers. The stories resonated with me because God worked through similar circumstances to call me to faith. These firsthand stories capture one common thread: When East meets West, they face curiosities or assumptions, trust or doubts, acceptance or refusal; both sides are compelled to think that only a miracle could help to overcome these obstacles. However, amidst the struggle and before they even become aware of his almighty hand at work, our Lord has already gotten the MESSAGE across. God's amazing grace through these encounters is so powerful that it not only brings light to the Chinese people but also fuels the faith of American missionaries. If you want to know what God is up to in the Middle Kingdom, I urge you to read this book.

*Prof. T. Z. Schwartz*
*Martin Luther College, New Ulm, MN*

Reading this book was like going to a Chinese restaurant and ordering dim sum: a collection of many small dishes that together make a wonderfully satisfying meal. *Open Doors, Open Hearts* serves as an inspiration to those who think only missionaries can go and spread the gospel. It serves to inspire each of us, that wherever we are we can find opportunities to share the gospel with others.

*Danny Wehmeyer*
*Vice Chairman, WELS Board for World Missions*

I was deeply moved. The teachers do a fantastic job describing the cultural differences and obstacles that need to be overcome when moving across the world to China and the overwhelming feeling that's so often, *How am I supposed to spread God's love when I can't even order dinner?! . . .* My heart was bursting as I read story after story of these lost, hopeless, miserable souls finding hope and love in Jesus. It's just absolutely incredible and inspiring to see how God's Word takes root and grows in hearts all over the world.

*Hannah Klusmeyer*
*Former volunteer teacher in China*

Poignant. . . . A great read. . . . The most meaningful pieces of the book for me had to do with a dichotomy familiar to those whose vocation it is to witness: the insecurity of a volunteer, not knowing if your work is good enough, set against the change of heart in individuals who hear the Word, not being able to thank you enough. What assurance this book provides, in first-person accounts, that God is in control and that his Word is powerful and will do what he intends it to do—through us, in us, even in spite of us!

*Karen Fischer*
*President, Lutheran Women's Missionary Society*

# OPEN
# DOORS
## OPEN HEARTS

# OPEN
# DOORS
# OPEN HEARTS

**Stories from the Mission Field in China**

Edited by Rachel Kamin
Foreword by Daniel Koelpin

**NORTHWESTERN PUBLISHING HOUSE**
Milwaukee, Wisconsin

Cover Photo: iStock
Interior Art: Shutterstock

Northwestern Publishing House
1250 N. 113th St., Milwaukee, WI 53226-3284
www.nph.net
© 2016 Northwestern Publishing House
Published 2016
Printed in the United States of America
ISBN 978-0-8100-2754-1

*For all teachers, past and present, who saw an open door and walked through it.*

# Contents

## Contents

# Acknowledgments

Thank you, teachers and students of the Word, for taking time out of your busy lives to write down your stories. Without your sense of urgency to share the gospel message to all ends of the earth, there would be no content to fill these pages. Many souls are being reached because of your lives of service.

Many thanks are also owed to both our mission organization and Northwestern Publishing House for seeing a great opportunity to shine a light and making it happen.

Thank you, Aaron, for your support and constant flow of input throughout this process. May God continue to bless your work in China.

Most importantly—God is so good. He has been our great Shepherd, watching over and blessing everyone involved in this project.

May this anthology give glory to God and be yet another seed that is planted in the hearts of many.

# Foreword

Jesus stated his life's mission when he said in the house of Zacchaeus, "For the Son of Man came to seek and to save the lost" (Luke 19:10). He included all of his followers in that mission for the lost when he gave his directive to "go and make disciples of all nations" (Matthew 28:19).

Being part of that mission floods the lives of believers with meaning and fulfillment. Guiding others to the truth of eternal life through Jesus begins in our families. It includes wives and husbands helping each other on the road to heaven and parents discipling their children in the way of faith. We often find even more participation in the mission of God as we reach out with the gospel to those we encounter in the course of day-to-day living. The Lord may bring us opportunity to share his saving Word with a hurting co-worker who has just lived through a crisis in life, a neighborhood family that has lost one of its own in death, or a close friend who has been recently hospitalized. Over the years, we begin to realize that all of this is part of our Savior's master plan for our respective roles in the evangelization of the world.

However, since most of us can't go to all locations in the world ourselves, we perceive our part in the *worldwide* mission as being done vicariously through others. We support and pray for missionaries who are willing to go to distant lands to share the truth of Jesus on our behalf. We do jointly with many other congregations and church members what we couldn't possibly do on our own—namely, sending to countries around the world those who are willing to go in our name. Thus, our part in the directive to reach out to the entire world has traditionally been done corporately, through our churches and church body.

Still, there have been times when believers have had opportunities to do mission work with foreigners more directly. We think of the incident of Philip and the traveling Ethiopian (Acts 8)—the account that weaves this anthology together—or the story of the displaced Israelite servant girl who was able to direct the Syrian commander Naaman to the prophet Elisha (2 Kings 5) or the time when the queen of Sheba traveled north to hear the wisdom of Solomon (1 Kings 10).

Today, though, the possibility of a church member or church worker doing direct mission work with foreigners has become greater than perhaps any other time in history. With globalization that is shrinking our planet, jet travel available to multitudes, technology that is able to leap oceans and borders, and mass migrations and immigrations occurring on a huge scale, our world has radically changed.

The experiences set forth in *Open Doors, Open Hearts* present us with heartwarming examples of this mission work. Around the turn of the century, China began to support American teachers of English as a Second Language (ESL) as part of its educational program. This development provided opportunity for scores of teachers from the United States to travel halfway around the world and become immersed in experiences that they would never have dreamed of in their wildest imaginations.

These are their stories. As you read them, you get glimpses of the New Testament being lived again in our time. Just as no one could have known that the humble meeting of the apostle Paul with women of Philippi (Acts 16) or the brief encounter between Philip and the Ethiopian would impact the proclamation of the gospel to distant countries and continents, so these teachers' gospel interactions with Chinese students and chance encounters with the people of China may have impact far beyond their humble beginnings.

When reading these accounts, there are a number of things that impress themselves upon us. We're impressed with how God can use chance encounters and everyday incidents to let our light shine and provide openings for gospel witness. We're fascinated with the fact that people very much like ourselves can share in the experiences of missionaries and walk in the footsteps of the apostle Paul. We're captivated by the hunger for the gospel that exists in other lands when we ourselves so often tend to take it for granted. Most of all, we are awestruck by the power of God's Word and sacrament and the effectiveness of prayer which are able to transcend the barriers of feeble witness, cultural obstacles, and language difficulties to produce amazing results in hearts and lives.

As one who has been involved in mission outreach in Asia for more than 30 years, I am convinced that our synod's Chinese mission program was part of God's plan for sharing the Good News in China. While teachers of English are not allowed to teach Christianity in the classroom, it is permissible for them to share their faith during off-hours with students. It is not going too far to say that this sharing of faith is even more fulfilling to these teachers than any of the academic accomplishments they may have in the classroom. Over the course of the last 15 years, thousands have studied the gospel and more than five hundred have been baptized.

We are grateful to the Lord for moving so many dedicated Christian teachers, called workers, and church members to leave the familiar comforts of US living and go halfway around the world to share the gospel. Their willingness to participate in this effort has truly been a leap of faith and a measure of personal sacrifice. Most of them would tell you, though, that what they lost in terms of comfort and convenience, they found in terms of joy and fulfillment as they shared the Good News and saw it take root. The Savior told his disciples, "No one who has left home or brothers or sisters or mother or father or children or fields for me and the gospel will fail to receive a hundred times as much in this present age . . . and in the age to come eternal life" (Mark 10:29,30). When losing our life for the gospel's sake, we find it.

The effort of our Chinese mission organization is ongoing and needs the support and prayers of Christians back home to cover recruiting costs, travel expenses, and the administration of the program. It is hoped that in reading the stories of these committed men and women we will see them as an arm of the church and provide such ongoing support as we are able.

*Daniel Koelpin*
*Former Mission Administrator*

# Editor's Preface

In 2009 I was blessed with the opportunity to move to Wuhan, China, to serve as a university English teacher. I joined up with our mission agency for some training and support prior to and during my time there. While I thoroughly enjoyed teaching English, I also couldn't ignore the strong pull toward the countless opportunities I had to tell the people of China about my Savior. Everywhere I turned, there were inquiring minds that were looking for someone to talk to. They may have heard about the Bible and were seeking a deeper meaning in their lives, or they may have just been looking for an English lesson from a Westerner. Whatever it was they bargained for, they ended up getting much more.

I remember considering myself ill-equipped to be a teacher of God's Word. I worried that I didn't know the Bible well enough to be able to adequately discuss it and answer all of the questions that came my way. However, I watched firsthand as the Holy Spirit grew seeds of faith all around me, regardless of how well I spoke. I often left conversations amazed at how evident it was that the words I had just spoken were not mine. God was using *me*, I realized. And he still is. I am thankful for my time in Wuhan and so honored to have been asked by the leaders of our mission agency to oversee this anthology.

Our title, *Open Doors, Open Hearts*, refers to the doors that are being thrown open all over China, allowing conversations about our Savior to enter into the lives and open hearts of so many curious people. It's common for evangelists in China to think, *I can't believe how easy that witnessing opportunity was.* Even so, we know these moments certainly aren't "easy" because of anything we are doing. The Holy Spirit is always there, guiding words and working faith.

When we first sent out a letter to our friends and evangelists asking if they would be willing to share their mission stories, we had no idea what kind of response we might get. Thank God that he had big plans for this project. Story after story rolled in, and soon we were sitting amidst an overabundance of written accounts from the mission field—a collection that could truly encompass the many different facets of the work being done in China.

The stories and letters that you will read in this anthology are from the mouths of those whose lives have been changed because of the work that the Holy Spirit is doing in China. These are the accounts of American teachers who have served or are still serving in cities across China. These are narratives by Chinese friends who met American teachers from our organization and want to share how blessed they feel to know God's truths. These are letters written by Chinese men and women for their Christian friends who have returned home to America, illustrating that although they have been separated by distance, the seeds of faith in their hearts are still being watered. I pray that the diversity of the authors in this book presents you with a richer depiction of personal experiences occurring every day in China.

As the overwhelming number of submissions poured in, I found that the stories categorized very naturally into six clear themes and that there were many parallels between these themes and the story of Philip and the Ethiopian from the book of Acts.

During my time in China, I often thought of the first words spoken between those two men: "'Do you understand what you are reading?' Philip asked. 'How can I,' he said, 'unless someone explains it to me?'" (Acts 8:30,31). This interaction seemed to simplify things for me as I walked the streets of China, surrounded by millions who had not yet had the opportunity to learn about Jesus. How truly un-complicated it was. I just needed to start sharing. I am thankful to be able to remind you of this account as it coincides with the stories in this book.

As you read, you'll notice the ambiguity used with each reference to the mission agency and church body that are represented in this book. Due to the fact that China still considers most organized church activity to be illegal, we need to ensure that our organization and all involved remain protected. Names of specific places and people have been changed or obscured. Each author is also kept anonymous. The authors were informed of the precautions being taken prior to sending in their submissions. I'd love to be able to give each of these talented people the credit they deserve, but instead I'm left awed by their humble and selfless hearts of service as they move the spotlight away from themselves and toward the greater purposes that this book serves.

Everyone who has had a hand in the creation of this anthology prays that this collection of stories and letters works far beyond the simple words that are written on each page. We pray that this book gets into as many hands as possible so that more may be enlightened about the hungry souls that need to be fed in China. We pray that these stories encourage those who may feel called to join this mission. If you are able—go! God will bless your work. And finally, we pray that after reading these stories, you are inspired. Whatever your walk in life, wherever your mission field, find open doors and walk through them. Build friendships. Watch as the Holy Spirit gives you strength you never knew you had.

God bless you.

*Rachel Kamin*

Now an angel of the Lord said to Philip, "Go south to the road—the desert road—that goes down from Jerusalem to Gaza." So he started out, and on his way he met an Ethiopian eunuch, an important official in charge of all the treasury of the Kandake (which means "queen of the Ethiopians"). This man had gone to Jerusalem to worship, and on his way home was sitting in his chariot reading the Book of Isaiah the prophet. The Spirit told Philip, "Go to that chariot and stay near it."

Then Philip ran up to the chariot and heard the man reading Isaiah the prophet. "Do you understand what you are reading?" Philip asked.

"How can I," he said, "unless someone explains it to me?" So he invited Philip to come up and sit with him.

This is the passage of Scripture the eunuch was reading:

"He was led like a sheep to the slaughter, and as a lamb before its shearer is silent, so he did not open his mouth. In his humiliation he was deprived of justice. Who can speak of his descendants? For his life was taken from the earth."

The eunuch asked Philip, "Tell me, please, who is the prophet talking about, himself or someone else?" Then Philip began with that very passage of Scripture and told him the good news about Jesus.

As they traveled along the road, they came to some water and the eunuch said, "Look, here is water. What can stand in the way of my being baptized?" And he gave orders to stop the chariot. Then both Philip and the eunuch went down into the water and Philip baptized him. When they came up out of the water, the Spirit of the Lord suddenly took Philip away, and the eunuch did not see him again, but went on his way rejoicing. Philip, however, appeared at Azotus and traveled about, preaching the gospel in all the towns until he reached Caesarea.

*Acts 8:26-40*

## Part One

## The Call

*Now an angel of the Lord said to Philip, "Go south to the road—the desert road—that goes down from Jerusalem to Gaza." So he started out. . . .*

# This Is Our Life

When I left the United States to teach in China, I was ready to give up my little Ford Fiesta and take on the public transportation of one of the biggest cities in China. Because I am older than the average teacher, I had prepared myself by hiking frequently and riding a mountain bike around my suburban neighborhood.

When I went to take the subway during rush hour that first morning in China, I felt confident. Along with a mass of people, I flowed through cattle gates and security screening, got carried up a flight of stairs, and then ran to my position "behind the yellow line." As I waited in queue, I watched employees called "pushers" do just that: push the backsides of people into already bursting train cars so that the doors could close.

Two trains later it was my turn. Once I was inside, I shifted—first my arm, then my head—so that I was no longer nose-to-nose with the guy beside me.

I must have sighed, because just then I heard, "This is our life!"

I turned my head to see a young Chinese professional

smiling at me. He was holding his arms and briefcase above his head, but he didn't seem distressed.

He started asking, in very good English, what I would soon discover to be common conversation-starting questions in China: "Where are you from?" "What is your job here?" and "How do you like the subway?" To conclude, he said again, "This is our life!"

This is our life.

Most of the non-students I have met so far are ones who have approached *me* while I've traveled back and forth between teaching jobs or while I've played with my two grandsons at the park or while I've attempted to walk my beautiful but unruly golden retriever. Everyone I meet shares the same goals: study extremely hard in order to stand out against thousands of other applicants for the best schools; find a good career and look forward to helping your parents as they age; and get married and have a child for Grandma and Grandpa to raise while you and your spouse work. *Duty* is China's god and source of happiness.

But, when I look deeper, I find more.

Twenty-five-year-old Ling moved to this city after college. She tells me she wasn't happy about the move, but her aunt requested her presence here, and her parents said yes. She was doing her duty and didn't argue that this would become her life. Ling's aunt heard about free English classes with our group. Both women attended, and both women learned some English. Ling, however, learned something more: on that very first day of English class, she "learned God." In the two years that followed, she learned the true meaning of her existence, and for the first time ever, she will tell you, she was happy.

Ling now dedicates her free time to Bible study and serving others. She has recently accepted a job with our day school as their accountant. Her parents, once leery of her new friends, her new outlook on life, and her meager paycheck, are slowly opening their hearts to the same "English lesson" that reached Ling. And Ling's aunt? She was baptized six months after Ling was and recently held her wedding in the church!

Ling's life has changed from one of blind duty with little hope to one of joyful service and eternal hope. She wakes with a smile and walks confidently on the same streets that carry so many hopeless souls. She points them out to me and says, "See, their heads are down, and they are not smiling. They do not have the happiness I have."

We don't stop with Ling, and we *can't* stop when God is constantly feeding more people to us! For example, "Andrea" (her English name that she chose) and my daughter-in-law Jenna met at a Western-style market that Andrea's in-laws own. Andrea comes to our study with her sister-in-law Nan. They are our most consistent attendees and bring many questions to the studies and ideas for fellowship to the group.

Then there's Cheng, who, after seeing the cross necklace

I was wearing, greeted me on the subway last fall. He wanted to practice his English, and we met several times for language lessons (and very awkward lessons they were, as he wanted to teach me Chinese at the same time!). However, he doesn't come to our Bible study often and, in fact, has just recently moved farther away. We continue to message each other, though, and hope to meet for a meal again before I head home. A seed has been planted, and I have to accept God's will and plan for Cheng. I pray *Thy will be done*, and I pray that I see this friend again in heaven.

Qiu overheard my son Eric and his friends doing a Bible study at a restaurant and asked if she could learn more. Now she is an energetic student and travels the greatest distance for a Sunday night class!

Kun is a coworker at my ESL school, and he brings his friend Rong to Bible study. Kun helps with a lot of in-class translation, and Rong and I are kindred souls and hope to go to a movie together soon.

Shen once saw me struggling with my golden retriever and started a conversation with, "Nice dog!" He is 34, doesn't have a full-time job, loves to play piano and Ping-Pong, and says he wants to improve his English, but . . . we're not sure where we stand with Shen right now. We haven't found all the spare time he requests from us to socialize, and he recently sent us this message: "I have been hurt by foreigners before, so I will stop coming." We continue to pray for him, and we look for opportunities to squeeze in some Ping-Pong!

Xiaoming and Fen are close neighbors to Eric and Jenna, and they have a small child. Many new Chinese parents look for help in raising their children. They see American children as well-behaved and disciplined in following schedules for eating and sleeping. Culturally, there's little training for that here, but many exhausted Chinese parents would like to make a change. Eric and Jenna enjoy sharing *Love and Logic* parenting ideals with these Chinese friends.

So, this is our life! I've learned that it's important to get out there, meet people, make friends, and share the Good News. I can't commit my whole day to playing Ping-Pong, but I can play a little. I know I need to be prepared for anything. I watch with amazement as his Word *works*.

I am thankful that this is my life in China.

# Not a Travelin' Man

I grew up in a small town in northern Ohio. We had exactly 256 residents. I know this because my friend Gary and I sat on a curb and counted them one hot, boring summer evening. Note that we never sat on the curb talking about traveling. Small towns didn't usually produce big adventurers who dreamed of going to far away countries.

I had no particular interest in going places to visit. I thought that maybe an occasional trip to Wisconsin might be okay. We had no hills in Ohio, and Wisconsin seemed to be a nice hilly area. But I couldn't imagine wanting to go much farther than that. I just never had a personal interest in going far. In fact, moving from one apartment to the next in our life made me homesick for our previous home. In Psychology 101 I learned that I liked homeostasis—the state of having things remain stable and relatively constant. I liked home. Traveling and moving upset that wonderful state.

But God intervened in my life. I met and fell in love with Laurie, and we got married. Not content to stay in one place, Laurie always had a hankering to travel.

Our first big trip had us packing our things and taking the whole summer to drive to Los Angeles and up the West Coast to Seattle and back to Wisconsin again, sightseeing all along the way. It was definitely the longest trip I had ever taken, and it was nice. I enjoyed many wonderful sights, and it became God's preparation for a few years later when we had the opportunity to move to California. We already knew a little bit of what it was like, and making the decision to go wasn't hard.

Laurie's travel plans for the following year took us to New Orleans for Easter, and that was the most exotic spot I had ever seen. I liked it.

Then a time came when a close friend gave us his left-over timeshares that Laurie wanted to use for a trip to Cancun, Mexico. That was a big step for me. Laurie still reminds me that when the timeshare nights ran out, I insisted on moving to a different hotel rather than buying some nights in our current hotel because the floor of the room was just tile and the shower had sand in it (a big step down from our home then, but a big step up from our current home in China). Laurie was bitten by the traveling bug, so we made two more vacation trips to Mexico.

The next few times we traveled, our daughters were also involved. We all went to Paris and Rome one year, followed by an extended trip to northern Italy the next year. A 14-day trip to Israel was another "Laurie idea," but it was a special thrill for me because we focused only on sites where Jesus had lived and visited.

God took me by the hand and little by little got me used to being in different countries, away from the comforts of home. But I was still a long ways away from wanting to pull up roots in Carlsbad, California, and move to rural China's coal-mining country, where Western comforts just don't exist and people generally speak only Mandarin.

Besides traveling for fun, Laurie was also always hoping to travel to South America to do some charitable work. I agreed that that would be an exciting thing to do, and we began looking for places where we could go and stay for a few weeks or months to help others.

God had other plans for us, though. Pastor Johnson, who was living in China, came to visit his brother, who happened to be my pastor in Carlsbad. While there, he taught and preached and spoke of the work being done in China. We learned that people were going there to teach English, being paid to do so by the Chinese government, and using their free time to spread the message of the Bible to the people in China. I told Laurie I was really interested in going, and she said, "Let's go! I'll support you."

So now the boy from small-town Ohio was hoping to head for China. Things sounded promising. However, our path to China had obstacles.

We contacted the head of our synod's Chinese mission agency, and he put us in touch with the organization's program director, Dan. Dan explained that they could really use someone with my pastoral background in Beijing, where the pastor there could use some help. So Dan put in an application to one of the schools in Beijing. Were we ever excited! Laurie, a lifetime librarian, grabbed my hand, and we headed for the bookstore to find books about China.

However, there is a policy in China that restricts the hiring of foreign teachers over the age of 60. I am indeed older than 60 (currently the oldest worker that this organization has ever sent to China), and a few weeks later we got the news from Dan that Beijing had said, "Sorry, you are too old."

Undeterred, Dan explained that Pastor Johnson could also use the help of someone with my background, since he was serving two cities in Zhejiang province. So we applied to teach there.

A few weeks later, their answer came back: "We're sorry, but you are too old." And so the story went on.

Dan applied for us in one city after another—six cities total. Each time the answer was, "We're sorry, but you are too old."

We got the message. China didn't want old teachers. Discouraged, we quit making plans for China, and we let our friends know that our plans had fallen through. We were embarrassed, too, because we had told our friends and acquaintances that we were going to China, not that we *might* be going to China. End of *that* story, it seemed—

—Not quite!

There was another city in the region of Ningxia that Dan had not yet tried. It was a small city that our mission agency had actually considered leaving in order to use those resources elsewhere. This was not as promising as other places in China. At about 230,000 people, it is currently one of the smallest cities in China in the smallest, poorest province in China. Anything smaller becomes a village. It is in the northern reaches of China, about ten miles from Inner Mongolia.

Because the city is small, any movements and activities by American residents are more obvious, making it more difficult to do mission work. The enforcers from State Administration for Religious Affairs are more active there, and they can see and hear from citizens what religious activities are going on. The province is considered poor and backwardly rural. The previous work done there through our organization had not produced many visible results. Current philosophy in our organization is generally to focus our personnel on highly populated areas where we can operate without being noticed so easily.

However, God had bigger plans for this city and us.

At that time, Kurt was one teacher from our organization that was living in this small city and had been for ten years. He was, and still is, a college and city fixture. Everyone seems to know Kurt, and he is considered an honored member of the school's staff. When our organization was talking about leaving this city, Kurt decided that he would stay even without backing and continue to teach at the school where he was employed. He was welcomed to do so by the school. Because of this, our organization decided to support him and keep this city as one of its sites, with Kurt being their only representative.

So Dan applied for teaching positions for us in this city. And when their answer came back, it was, "Yes, we would like to have you teach here."

Our emotions had to do another 180-degree turn. It was hard and confusing, but we were excited. We started making plans to rent out our American house for a year. Little did we know our time in China would be much longer than one year and filled with endless stories of God's love and grace!

# How Can They Hear?

The Lord can truly transform hearts. That is the only explanation for how I ended up leaving the home I loved and spending a year halfway across the globe. It was something more than curiosity that led my husband and me to attend a lecture being given by a man on the teaching opportunities available in China. It was certainly the Lord's hand at work. We both entered the room with no desire whatsoever to teach in China. Little did we know how our hearts would feel when we left that room.

We listened first with polite interest and later with intensity as we heard about the growing number of Chinese Christians. We were told that the door to China is open now. The Chinese people have a great interest in learning the English language. They want native English speakers to teach them. Teachers who are Christians are welcomed because they are seen by the Chinese as honest, reliable people. As teachers who are Christians live and work among the Chinese people, there are many opportunities for witnessing about Jesus, our Savior, who was sent for all nations. The Chinese government will not allow foreign pastors to live in China and "preach" to the people, but the door is open to do "friendship evangelism." The Lord has been greatly blessing this work. We listened all the more intently as we heard stories and saw the smiling photos of Chinese people who had become Christians through the witness of English teachers.

At one point, something like scales fell off my hardened heart. Scripture verses began swirling through my mind: "And everyone who calls on the name of the LORD will be saved" (Joel 2:32) and "How, then, can they call on the one they have not believed in? And how can they believe in the one of whom they have not heard? And how can they hear without someone preaching to them? And how can anyone preach unless they are sent? As it is written: 'How beautiful are the feet of those who bring good news!'" (Romans 10:14,15).

After the scales fell off, a burning desire burst forth in my heart to go and tell people in China about Jesus, the Savior. The same sort of thing happened in my husband's heart, because we both left that room saying, "Maybe we could do that next year?"

# Letter From China

*Hello Mike,*

*I am interested in Jesus more and more now! Before now, I think Jesus is just a great man and just for Christians. But now I find the Spirit of Jesus is suitable for all people, all over the world. If everyone believe Jesus, the world will keep peace and more beautiful. Right?*

*The USA is the strongest country in the world nowadays, but China has more than 5,000 years history and #1 population in the world. I think if we, Chinese and Americans, understand each other completely and respect each other and become good friends, the world will be more and more beautiful, and no conflict, no war, and people live a happy and safe life. I think Jesus would like that world, don't you?*

*So I will try my best to learn the Bible, and I hope you can learn the Chinese culture. We belong to the world, too. I look forward to seeing you soon. Enjoy and cherish every day!*

*Your friend,*

*Liu*

# Part Two

# The Curiosity

*. . . and on his way he met an Ethiopian eunuch, an important official in charge of all the treasury of the Kandake (which means "queen of the Ethiopians"). This man had gone to Jerusalem to worship, and on his way home was sitting in his chariot reading the Book of Isaiah the prophet. The Spirit told Philip, "Go to that chariot and stay near it."*
*Then Philip ran up to the chariot and heard the man reading Isaiah the prophet. . . .*

# Shining Bright

Accompanied by a popular pop song, "Sun" strode to the front of the room to receive his award at an annual gathering of Chinese and American friends this past May. His award—really just an excuse to celebrate some personal quirk or story from the past year—was the first ever New Einstein of the Year Award. Yeah, he's a smart guy.

I had no idea how apt his English name was when I first met him. We became friends within my first few weeks in Beijing at a restaurant near my community.

"Nǐhǎo," I said to this complete stranger as I caught his eye a few feet away.

"Hello," he said back to me in comparatively better English.

Soon, instead of eating alone, we each had a tablemate. By the end of lunch, we had one another's phone numbers. We connected on social media.

We continued to meet for lunch or dinner once every week or so. Food is an awesome thing to share with someone—especially if, like me, you enjoy trying new things. But I had something more than just an aptitude for adventurous fare to share with Sun. Meal times for most Christians are opportunities to publicly give thanks. For Sun and me, our meal times together were opportunities to let the candle of faith burn brightly. They were a chance to shine light. They were the beginning of Sun's path to real sight.

Sun eventually joined my men's Bible study group. He didn't know what to think of the Bible at first. He enjoyed my friendship, to be sure, but this stuff about God? In his own words, "At the first beginning, I am curious about everything and a little bit scared about whether you guys will share some bad things. I am also doubting about what you said. So during the study, too many questions troubled me."

Though a little scared and doubtful, Sun remained always respectful. He listened, asked questions, and made us think. We continued to grow closer in our friendship, and this allowed for more opportunities to share the light of Christ.

I thank God for Sun, and I would thank God even if our story ended there. But, thanks to God, it doesn't. Not long after I met Sun, after time spent with us as friends and time spent together in the Bible, his heart opened.

He had these thoughts to share: "After a few months of study and a few activities with brothers, I came to like the words in Bible. Especially it's amazing that Jesus took all the sin for us because he loved us. He is a really perfect man. God sacrificed himself for the human being. I still know too little about God and Bible, and many questions still confuse me. But I think I will continue studying Bible in the future, as I trust Jesus who is the only one to save us."

Though in his estimation he knew too little, Sun had something more precious than knowledge—even Einstein's. Though still confused, he understood the truth. Though perhaps still doubting, he trusted. For the first time in his life, Sun was truly seeing. He had real light. Sun had Jesus.

Sun spoke the truth that was in his heart, but he didn't need to. We could *see* it. His faith lit up the room. It shined bright as he eagerly attended each study, welcomed new-comers, sought (and found) answers, and became our brother in faith. His light—a reflection of the light of the gospel—was impossible to miss. Sun was living up to his name. He was shining brightly for all to see.

Shining in the darkness isn't always easy, though. While a foreigner Christian in China is generally accepted and expected, a Chinese Christian is often subject to ridicule and persecution. Even friends may make fun because they can't understand why Jesus has any place in a young Chinese person's life. This has been Sun's experience.

"Even now I am struggling with this," Sun remarks, "but I am not afraid of that, as he is carrying me to walk all the way."

And God certainly is carrying him. Inspired by Chinese brothers mature in faith and his 85-year-old grandmother who looks forward to her heavenly home, Sun continues to open his Bible and his song book to learn God's words and sing God's praise. God continues to feed his flame of faith.

We are now nearing the end of our second year together as friends and brothers. Sun is as faithful as ever in our study together, and whether he knows it or not, he has become a leader among our brothers, shining the light of a faith grown by the Holy Spirit. After I go home, he will continue to be at the core of a group of Chinese brothers studying the Word. He will feed his faith, and by God's grace it will burn brighter.

And as this fire grows, God will shine through Sun to bring light to others still in darkness. Sun's mother and father and family back home still do not know of the light of Christ. Sun recently married, and his wife, though she knows of his faith, still does not know Jesus herself. Also, Sun will soon be a daddy, and this is a gift for which we can't give enough thanks. He will have the chance to light the candle of faith in a new, young life. God has set Sun on fire, and by his grace Sun will continue to light the lives of those around him, and those after him, with the Everlasting Light.

Shine bright, Sun.

# The Power of a Prayer

It was a meal like many others. The waitress set menus and miniature cups of steaming hot green tea on the table and eyed us curiously. Our illiteracy led us to shun the menu and rattle off a few of our favorite dishes to the young *fúwùyuán*. She scribbled a character or two on her thin notepad and left us to our tea and company: the obligatory portrait of Chairman Mao, a golden Buddha statuette that graced most restaurants, and the most noteworthy, Mei. Mei was a bright, quiet young woman who was usually overshadowed by her loud, long-haired boyfriend, Qing. Qing was absent that day, so we looked forward to getting to know Mei more. Before long, our *xiǎo bái cài* (Chinese cabbage), *fānqié chǎo jīdàn* (fried tomatoes with eggs), and marquee dish *Wǔchāng yú* (fish smothered in red hot peppers), were set before us. We folded our hands on the flimsy plastic tablecloth, bowed our heads, and quietly spoke, "Come, Lord Jesus . . ."

Weeks went by, and we continued to make other ac-quaintances and deepen many different friendships. So regularly did the Lord provide opportunities to invite these new friends to our apartment to study the Word, and so often did they gladly accept our invitations, that it almost became the exception when someone declined.

Mei, though a bit shy, was certainly a top prospect. We were sure it wouldn't be long before she was not only a friend but a sister in Christ. Yet, having never accepted our invitation to study with us, she became an exception.

Another meal with Mei ended, and we began the long walk to her bus stop. Passing our building on the way, we climbed the three flights of stairs for a brief hiatus in our apartment before she went on her way.

We entered our 400-square-foot home and sat down— Mei in a comfortable corner chair. From there she asked, "Do you have a Bible?"

The answer was easy, and soon she was flipping open the green butterfly cover to page 1 of the bilingual New Testament. And she read. No doubt many questions crossed her mind, but for the next two hours, only a few crossed her lips. Our answers were brief because Mei wasn't so much interested in what we had to say as in what the author of that book was saying. Whether it was the realization that she had been quietly reading in our apartment for the better part of the afternoon or something else, eventually Mei broke away from the book.

"Keep it," we said. We also had the gumption to ask why, after all this time, she decided she needed a Bible.

Her response? "Do you remember the first time we ate

together? The spicy fish? I remembered you prayed. This made me curious, so I started to do some research."

We'd spent months of strategizing how to penetrate this "exception," but it had already been done. The words of our prayer—even just the fact that we had folded hands and bowed heads—piqued Mei's curiosity. The seed had been planted, and the only one who could make it grow was already hard at work in his garden.

# Coffeehouse Ministry

"Will you teach us the Bible?"

That question was an answer to many months of prayers! It had seemed so long in coming, but of course it was exactly God's timing all along.

My wife and I were a part of the first team in our Hubei city of eight million people. We were sent by our mission agency with few instructions—it was a new city, after all, and a relatively new mission field for any of us. "May the Lord be with you!" was our founder's parting message to us.

When we landed, we were relieved to be greeted by representatives of our school. The apartments weren't ready yet, they told us. Not a problem—we would stay in a hotel for a while. The bigger dilemma for us non-Chinese speakers was the apparent lack of English speakers in our district. For the first few weeks, our team wondered whether we were in the wrong part of our city. How would we make relationships with such a significant language barrier?

One of the first, most tangible answers to prayer came through an invitation from one of our Chinese colleagues. She asked if we would like to join her at an English coffeehouse about an hour away by bus. Of course we accepted the invitation, and not just because we found out they also served tacos! When we arrived, we learned that this particular coffeehouse was owned and operated by a Christian couple from Louisiana who felt called by God to create a meeting place for God's people to connect with one another and with English-speaking Chinese.

What a blessing this place turned out to be! In our two years, we probably made the commute over 50 times. We were able to connect with one new friend after another. Sure, the questions got a little old sometimes. Yes, we can use chopsticks, and yes, we can say a couple words in Chinese! But their curiosity was understandable. They didn't often have the opportunity to talk with foreigners.

It wasn't long into these conversations, though, that something divine happened. These friends opened up to us. They asked questions, listened intently, and shared their thoughts about their country and families and work. And more often than not, we had opportunities to share our spiritual worldview with them—a worldview that considers this life to be a life *before* life—a life of hope and forgiveness in Jesus. And they *received it*, just as God promised when he assured us his Word would not return to him empty.

It was about December of our first year, four months after our arrival. We were at this coffee shop, engaged in conversation, when two friends approached us. "Will you teach us the Bible?" they asked.

We began our first formal study the very next week. My wife and I were invited to meet in the apartment of one of these men—two of us with four Chinese friends. It was a tiny apartment, with the bedroom functioning as the living room and the six of us sitting on rock-hard twin beds facing each other. And from that space we pored through our Great Exchange tracts and the book of Mark and the Old Testament forefathers, sipping hot water from paper-thin plastic cups and snacking on some kind of raisin we never did develop a taste for.

By God's grace, we outgrew that space. Seeing opportunities for ministry in a more central part of town, we considered renting an apartment to be used exclusively for Bible studies. Our teammates had use for it too, as we were now meeting about four nights a week for various Bible studies.

It was about that time that our good friends from our synod's church in Big Bend, Wisconsin, sent a mission offering to support our work—enough to rent an apartment for an entire year and furnish it too! *It's a God thing*—a phrase we repeated often.

We rented a space about four times bigger than our friend's original apartment and furnished it with couches, chairs, and bookshelves for our growing library. Seeing no sense in leaving it empty during the day, we let a couple friends live in it rent-free. We gave them a water heater that Christmas—and to think this was only one year after that initial invitation to study at our friend's apartment!

One of the original members was a medical doctor who fittingly chose "Luke" as his English name. He attended every Bible study we offered and absorbed every word his limited English would allow. He took us to visit his family and peppered us with questions about the pain and suffering in this world. He took us to soccer games with his dictionary and Bible and asked us to help him understand biblical words and concepts. He continues to be one of the most faithful members to this day.

God has truly blessed this city. There are two house churches* now, each with Chinese pastors trained by our seminary in Hong Kong. Luke attends one of them—a fellowship that had its roots in his curiosity over a decade ago.

It's an amazing and humbling experience to be used by God in such visible ways. His kingdom work happens on *his* time, at exactly the right time. To God be the glory, for from him and to him and through him are all things.

---

*The Chinese government recognizes and sanctions only one official Christian church. This "registered" church body is officially named the Three-Self Patriotic Movement, as it is required to be self-supporting, self-governing, and self-propagating (i.e., free from outside influence like foreign missionaries or other religious groups).*

*Not surprisingly, the church is subject to governmental influence and suffers from significant doctrinal inconsistency. For these reasons, Chinese*

## The Curiosity

*Christians often seek fellowship and teaching from outside the registered church.*

*All organized Christian activities that take place outside of the registered church are, by definition, unregistered and illegal. The "house church" movement is a broad term that covers all these unregistered activities. House churches and other unregistered fellowships can range in size from just a few people in a rural living room to several thousand gathering in an urban rented space. Generally speaking, the government allows these unregistered groups to continue operating as long as they do not get too large or politically influential.*

*The house churches have experienced significant growth in recent years. Even the most conservative estimates now show that there are more Christians practicing outside the registered church than within it. Nevertheless, house church leaders and their members are ever mindful of security and often experience their own social or cultural persecution as a result of being associated with these groups.*

# You Lighten Our Life

"You lighten our life because you bring Jesus to us." These are the words I remember when I'm asked about my years in China.

I remember the first few days of orientation as if they were yesterday. Up until that point, I had never been abroad. I was fresh out of college and, after some amazing years of ministerial education and ministry experiences, I was feeling God's hand leading me to China. As I sat in my chair during the orientation seminars, I could hardly sit still. I was *going to China* and would be used to change lives forever with the message of Jesus! Needless to say, I was excited. Yet, it wasn't until two years later as I looked back on my experiences in China that I realized how humbling this ministry could be.

I remember those first few months in China. New home, new city, new foods, new smells (and I mean *new* smells), and, of course, new friends. One of those friends was Chin. I remember the first time Chin came to our men's Bible study and how skeptical he was. Sure, he probably came just to make foreign friends or improve his English, but he kept coming. I got to know Chin really well those first few months, and as time went on, the questions he'd ask were *definitely* not your typical "I'd-like-to-improve-my-English" questions. Chin was struggling—struggling to identify himself in a city of 20 million people, struggling to stand under the weight of Chinese male expectations for success, and buckling under the pressures of China's intense academic competition. Chin was searching for a constant—a *peace*—that would calm the storms in his life. Oddly enough, this peace was searching for him too, and it found him and called him by name.

The first time we sang "When Peace Like a River" at Bible study, the words cut to Chin's heart.

> *When peace like a river attendeth my way,*
> *When sorrows like sea billows roll—*
> *Whatever my lot, thou hast taught me to say,*
> *It is well, it is well with my soul.*
>
> *My sin—oh, the bliss of this glorious thought—*
> *My sin, not in part, but the whole,*
> *Is nailed to the cross, and I bear it no more:*
> *Praise the Lord, praise the Lord, O my soul!*
>
> *And, Lord, haste the day when my faith shall be sight,*
> *The clouds be rolled back as a scroll;*
> *The trump shall resound, and the Lord shall descend;*
> *Even so, it is well with my soul.*

With tears in his eyes, Chin belted out these words. At every men's study after that, Chin requested that we sing that song. It became the anthem for the brothers of our men's study, but especially an anthem for Chin.

If you haven't already guessed, Chin is a pretty emotional guy. Because of that, I knew he needed a bit more one-on-one time than any other member of my Chinese family.

One day, I sat down with Chin and asked about his day. The conversation that followed is something I will never forget.

He said, "Today our professor asked us two really interesting questions."

"What questions?" I asked.

"He asked us to write down the top three things we need to bring with us wherever we go and the most influential teacher in our life."

I was sensing that Chin was setting up for a good joke. "What did you write down, Chin?" I asked with a smile on my face, readying myself to laugh.

The first thing he said that he needed to bring everywhere was a phone, just in case he would ever get lost. The second was his wallet, so he could pay for food. His third answer, however, caught me completely off guard.

"The Bible," he said.

Chin clearly wasn't making jokes.

"What made you decide to bring the Bible, Chin?"

"Because it is the Word of God, and I need that. Do you know who I wrote for the most important teacher in my life?"

"Who did you write?"

"Jesus," he said.

Wow.

As our friendship grew, Chin also continued to grow. I remember his excitement when he told me about what Bible stories he was reading *on his own*. I remember the first time I heard him vocally pray to God. I remember the first time he called Jesus his Savior. Faith had not only taken root in his heart, but the fruits of faith were exploding off his spiritual tree.

I remember my mood one Saturday as I was riding my bike to our Bible study group's Thanksgiving dinner. I had just experienced a rather difficult week. I wasn't feeling particularly great about myself or my abilities as an evangelist that day. As I biked to that Thanksgiving dinner, I wasn't thinking about what things I was thankful for.

During the meal, I placed my friend's video camera on the table's lazy Susan and told everyone that I had an idea to make a Thanksgiving video. The plan was that I would spin the lazy Susan with the camera on it, and as the camera pointed at each of my brothers, they would get a chance to tell God in prayer one thing they were thankful for. One by one, brothers whom I had grown very close to through men's study shared an abundance of things they were thankful for, including blood-bought redemption through Jesus. I was blown away.

When the camera fell to Chin, he gave the most awesome testimony I had ever heard from him, and he prayed to God with confidence, "You are the Way, the Truth, and the Life."

And then the camera fell to me.

I went to China eager to be God's tool to change lives. I had no idea that God would use my Chinese brothers to change *me*. My time in China was filled with many adventures: dinners at dingy restaurants, overnight trains, the best noodles in the world, boating up the Li River, deep-fried dumplings, the joys of studying and speaking Mandarin, the burn of *báijiǔ* liquor, and even being a groomsman at a friend's wedding. But not one of those experiences can come even close to seeing firsthand what God is doing in China. To see a life go from completely void of Christ to revolving around him so much that he becomes "the most influential teacher in your life" is forever humbling and downright mind-blowing.

As the camera faced me, I looked at the faces around the table and said exactly that. I thanked God for growing my brothers in the faith, for giving me the chance to share Jesus with them, and for bringing my new friends into my life. Seeing those men gather weekly around God's Word and the truths within it made me so, so thankful.

I hadn't finished my prayer when Chin jumped in,

saying what forever defined my time in China—"You lighten our life because you bring Jesus to us."

The day before I left China, I, along with my other men's study brothers, went to a recording studio and recorded ten songs, one of them being "When Peace Like a River." The first time I heard the recording, it brought me to tears. I didn't have to strain too hard to pick out Chin's voice. God is eternally good.

# Good Question

One December day, two of my students stayed after English class to talk to me. They were both girls around 16 years old. I still don't know why they had been thinking of death. Perhaps someone they knew had recently died. Or perhaps they had been thinking of the words of a Christmas song I was teaching them about the meaning of the Christmas tree. The song ended with the words, "In Christ we, like the evergreen, will live forevermore."

At any rate, they were thinking of death, and they stayed behind to talk with me privately. "What do people in America say when someone dies?" they asked.

I told them that most of the people I knew in America were Christians. When someone died, we were sad because we missed that person, but we also had hope that we would see them again in heaven with Jesus. I told them simply how God had sent his Son, Jesus, to die for everyone's sins and that whoever believed in Jesus would live forevermore in heaven. In heaven, there would be no more sickness, sadness, pain, or death. Jesus proved he had power over death because he himself came alive after being dead.

These girls were both fairly good English speakers, but with English not being their native tongue, I was not sure if they would understand. I was very careful to use words I hoped they knew, and I asked them if they understood or if there was anything they wanted me to explain again. They both said they understood what I had said.

Then I asked them, "What do people in China say when someone dies?"

They both looked at each other as if at a loss for words. Finally one of them told me, "People just cry a lot."

These girls knew nothing except a grief that had no hope. I told them of a hope they had never heard of before. I told them about the only hope there is: Jesus. After another one of our classes, these same girls asked if I would make them a tape of the Christmas songs I had been teaching them. I gladly did that for them and provided them with a printout of all the words to the songs. Then several other students also wanted copies of the songs. Most Chinese have heard of Christmas, but they think it is like their Spring Festival—just a time for a holiday and to be with family. It is my prayer that these students left my class knowing Christmas is about Jesus, our hope in grief.

# Letter From China

*Morning Peter,*

*When I read Bible this morning, Psalms 3, wow so encouraging. I thought thanks Peter for pushing me to do this in my heart. I wasted a lot of time before. I hope it's not too late. I still have one question—you know when I read Bible, the knowledge of Bible will grow, but how can I make it personal? I mean how can I communicate with God, not just have the knowledge. How can I get real interaction? Different people have different stuff to deal with, so personally what does God want to teach me or show me or guide me?*

*Kind regards,*

*Ming*

(The day after Ming's baptism . . .)

*Yes, sir, Peter, I am just so happy, like a child gets a favorite toy or candy! I want to dance.*

*Ming*

## Part Three

# The Uncertainty

*. . . "Do you understand what you are reading?" Philip asked. "How can I," he said, "unless someone explains it to me?" So he invited Philip to come up and sit with him. . . .*

# Just Be Patient

My husband and I arrived in China with just a few Mandarin words in our vocabulary, including *xièxie* ("thank you") and *bīng shuǐ* ("iced water")—words taught to us by a helpful fellow traveler on the flight over. Thankfully, we soon met a Chinese language teacher, Xiaolan, who gave us a few lessons. As we got to know her, we shared what we were doing in China and our Christian faith. We learned that she was a Buddhist. She described her religion as a beautiful religion and would sometimes pray at Buddhist temples in the city and in other countries as she traveled.

We weren't alone in trying to reach Xiaolan with the gospel. She had taught Mandarin to many teachers before and after us, and everyone shared their faith with her in some way. I also heard the story that on one train ride, Xiaolan sat between two pastors! God's Word was surrounding her, but for some reason she never came to a Bible study or seemed interested. We never stopped praying that her heart would be opened and that she would one day believe.

A couple of years after we left China, Xiaolan got a job

teaching Chinese in the United States. We were able to visit her and also invited her to meet our families at Thanksgiving. She attended a few church services with us, and I gave her a Bible as a gift. Still, she seemed to show no interest in God's Word. Thankfully, she never completely closed the door on conversations about God, and she remained a close friend.

Seven years after we were first in China, we were able to go back for a visit. Xiaolan was back in China by then, married and with a son, and we arranged to get together with her. During that visit, we again tried to bring our faith into conversations. We discussed the amazing message of redemption through Jesus and her family's need for this Savior. Her husband had studied a little of the Old Testament in college but didn't consider himself a Christian. We prayed for his heart to open as well. We left China with constant prayers on our hearts for Xiaolan and her family. We had been praying for seven years, and we weren't giving up!

Then one day I got a voice message from her. She said she had seen a play about the life of Jesus. She had always loved theater, and for some reason this play affected her. In the voice message, she talked about the amazing story of Jesus and said that she had started reading the Bible because of this play! She talked about a change in how she felt, and she started asking questions about the Bible.

When I heard that message, I literally danced around

the room in joy! After almost eight years of praying for Xiaolan, God had opened her heart to hear the truth of his Word.

I still pray for her and her family. Being so far away, it is difficult to guide her and help her find the scriptural answers she is looking for. My prayer is that she will connect with Christians in her city and regularly search the Scriptures. I pray that her faith will take root and the light of Jesus will shine on her family members to open their hearts as well.

Above all, I desperately want to see them in heaven one day, along with all of our dear friends and as many Chinese men, women, and children as possible. The harvest is truly ripe! I can't think of any other place in the world right now where people are becoming Christians in such numbers. This is a window of opportunity to share the gospel that we just can't ignore.

# Give It Another Look

My husband and I had a friend that said he had read the Bible, but he could not believe it. He hoped that we would still be friends with him even though he was not a Christian. We assured him that we would still like to be friends with him.

One night the man invited us out to eat. At the end of the evening, after dinner, we shared a taxi ride home. As we were departing the taxi, he told us the reason he could not accept the Bible. He said he had read about how God had led the people of Israel out of Egypt, and he could not believe in a god who would kill people's children. Since he said this as we were parting for the night, and since he had gotten drunk (a sin which is a common struggle in China during social gatherings), the moment was not right for us to try to respond to him.

My husband was very disturbed by the man's comments because it was an argument he had heard before. He knew that it was time to wrestle with this barrier to faith, so he stayed up late and prayerfully wrote a letter to the man. He explained that the man did not understand everything that had happened before the exodus. He wrote about how the Egyptians had been killing not just the firstborns of Israel, but every male child that was born. He also explained that through the plagues, God had given the Egyptian pharaoh many chances to repent of his evil. He further went on to explain that all people are evil and deserve eternal death. He said that God is just, but he is also loving and gives people a way out of the eternal punishment they deserve. That way out is Jesus. Everything that happened in the Old Testament was pointing to the New Testament. When God told the people of Israel to paint the blood of the lamb on their doorposts, it was foreshadowing Jesus, who would shed his blood for all people.

The man was very grateful to receive the letter. He was amazed that my husband had taken the time to write to him personally. He said he realized now that he did not understand all that had happened and that he needed to give the Bible another look. So, we invited him to attend our Friday night Bible classes. He faithfully attended. Since he knew English the best in that group, he did most of the translating throughout the studies. His wife was going to university in another province, but when she was back in town for vacations, he brought her along to the Bible classes.

We took him and the others through the basics of Scripture. We started with creation, the fall into sin, and the first promise of the Savior. Then we went through the birth of Jesus, some of his miracles, his death, and his resurrection.

## The Uncertainty

We went through the meaning of justification and the peace and eternal life Jesus offers us. It was the first time anyone had given them a clear overview of the Bible. Before we left China, they were concerned about who would continue teaching them. They were all very glad when we told them that our replacements would also be Christians who would be happy to teach them the Bible. Praise the Lord for allowing our organization to continue working in this city to this day.

# David

I was born and raised in northeast China. My family is Christian, so I know a lot of God's words from Mom. David was the first name that came to my eyes when I opened my Bible for the first time. Then I gave myself English name "David" (I know nothing of this guy).

But I never read Bible and go to church. In my heart it's so empty, tensed, peaceless for many years. I never figured out why. I really wonder how did I spend the horrible years before I study God's words?

After graduation, I have a strong desire to come to Beijing. (Don't ask me why, because I don't know either.) My parents persisted in keeping me home through arguing, but then I was allowed to go with a promise to go to church once I reach Beijing.

I failed interview for three months again and again. I never forgot how painful. I questioned myself rubbish.

I decided to suicide one night, but I seemed to know from my mom that self-murder will lead to hell? I was very afraid. I felt desperate for death like I had no choice, but thank God, he stopped me.

I prayed for one hour, then I fell asleep.

God answered my prayer, giving me a job, and I knew many good friends. I felt so great so I stopped praying and worshiping.

Then I went to my friends' apartment. I was impacted by them. My life turned upside down. I took my first cigarette and high degree wine. I go to night bars. I know many unbelievers. My life became absolutely different, just to please them. In my heart, it seems so hurt, so empty, and it still can't be filled.

I tried to make my heart comfortable, but I failed. I felt lonely even though so many friends around me. My life couldn't be more horrible. I could focus on nothing, and I quit my job. Then I sought jobs again. I almost spent all my money. At the same time I was hurt by my friends. I had nothing, so I pray again, "God, you don't love me anymore?"

I hesitated, and then I decided to suicide again. I walked upon the bridge, watching the cars, wondering what if I jumped off and everything was over.

But when I wanted to jump, my leg didn't work. It was stiff and I couldn't walk. I know God loves me and thank him for stopping me.

But things did not change. I lived in bad surroundings, smoking, drinking wine. One night my friends drove off and I was home alone. I wanted to suicide again. I was desperate. I cried. I felt sorry.

"God, you make me righteous, but I choose unrighteousness. Sorry, Dad, Mom, sister, my friends. I am a bad son, a bad brother. Bye, my friends." I prepared to take the knife, but my heart beated more quickly than normal. When I saw blood drops, I didn't have the courage. God loves me, and I thank him for stopping me again.

Then I prayed every day. Every Sunday I went to church, and I read Bible every day.

Then I have the story of my American brother Caleb. I think it is no accident to meet Caleb. Since I came to his study, my heart full of peace. The feeling I never got before. I never found Bible and God's words so powerful.

It seemed everything in Bible was written for me. Then I realized that studying with Caleb and other Christians can make my life light. They build me up. God's love attracts me. I found comfort there.

Now I have a strong desire to study every day. It seems studying is my whole life.

I know so many passages in the Bible from Caleb and other teachers. So many beautiful words. They are the power from God.

When I experience the sufferings now and know God's love, I can't allow myself to go the old way.

My favorite passage in Bible is "We are more than conquerors through him who loved us. For I am convinced that neither death nor life, neither angels nor demons, neither the present nor the future, nor any powers, neither height nor depth, nor anything else in all creation, will be able to separate us from the love of God that is in Christ Jesus our Lord" (Romans 8:37-39).

I am thankful to Caleb. God saved me and healed me. God is the medicine, and Caleb has been the needle to me. I knew from Caleb that God brings me closer to him with my sufferings. His unfailing love can't be earned.

# Have I Done Enough?

During my first year in China, I had the wonderful opportunity to travel far from my home in the big city of Beijing to the western part of China to visit our team in the relatively rural region of Ningxia. I was excited for this travel experience because I could spend time with fellow American missionaries whom I had met during our month of training prior to coming to China and in the meantime get to see the work that the Lord had given them to do in a very different environment than what I was adjusting to in Beijing.

Upon arrival in Ningxia, I was excited to see the excitement and opportunities for ministry that were being showered on this team as well. I met several of their friends and attended a handful of studies. As we were just approaching a holiday and many friends were going home to see family, one of the other Christian teachers and I made plans to visit one of her good friends, Ting, in the deep countryside. Ting had been attending Bible studies for several months and had been touched greatly by the message of love found in God's Holy Word. She would often compare this "loving God" to the god she knew in her Islamic background. Ting was raised as a Muslim, and until she met our team of Christian teachers, she knew very little about the truth of Jesus and the forgiveness we have through his sacrifice on the cross. Over this holiday week, Ting was excited to lead two of her American friends to her hometown to share this good news with her family.

Ting's hometown was in a very rural area. The experience for me was like none other. Children played with metal rings and old oil filters as they pushed them with sticks taken from the trees. Shepherds were seen looking after their flocks and tending to the sheep that were injured. We were able to talk to one old shepherd as he braced one of his sheep's broken legs with a simple wooden splint and strips of cloth. Young women gracefully and seemingly effortlessly carried water from the town's well on a bamboo rod laid across their shoulders. I tried to help with this but found that more water splashed out of the two buckets than stayed in them by the time I returned to the home. We cooked on outdoor wooden fireplaces and ate and slept in homes dug out of the hillside. This was my first (and only) experience living in a cave. Life was different for Ting and her family.

The home we stayed in was that of Ting's older sister. This older sister had five children, and, though she lived in a cave dug from the hillside, her family was considered one of the wealthiest in the village. Her husband was a leader at the mosque and thus was honored by many in the surrounding areas. Their wealth and status was shown in the fact that the family had a motorcycle to use to get from one place to another; most families depended solely on their feet for transportation. This family was also devoutly religious to the god Allah. During my time with the family, I slept in the same room as the mosque's elder while my fellow American friend slept in a room with Ting, her sister, and the five children. Each night I was there I was awakened by the evening and early morning prayers they offered to their god. Truthfully, it was this grip on falsehood that made my stay the most uncomfortable. I too prayed (to the one true God) that their family might hear and receive the message of truth.

My American friend and I had plenty of time to talk with Ting and, through translation, with Ting's sister and the kids. I found myself struggling to really communicate what was pressing on my heart but found it easy to simply play with the kids and show them how much I loved them. Of course I wanted them to know how much God loved them and how he had sent Jesus to be their Savior, but that just didn't seem to come out as easily as playing tag and "Duck, Duck, Goose." By the end of our short three-day stay, I was feeling that I had let the children down. I felt I should have focused more of my time on the most important message—Jesus—and less time on games and fun. I consoled myself by thinking, *You can't speak their language and they can't speak a word of English so you don't have to worry about it*, yet I worried about it. I knew their natural condition (sinful like all people), and I knew the result of sin and the consequence of life without Jesus. I was not feeling very good.

Our time came to leave, and we all walked about a mile to the roadside to catch a random bus that would bring us into town. My fellow American missionary was having a conversation with Ting and her sister while I stuck close to the children. The kids kicked dust into the air as they walked, their faces downcast as they anticipated our departure.

And then I heard something I will never forget. One of the younger children—she was maybe six years old—turned to me and said in English as clear as could be, "Thank you for sharing Jesus with us."

These children could not speak English. Not even "hello" was in their vocabulary. Yet with my own ears I heard these beautiful words from this child's mouth. I was amazed. I turned at once to my American friend and asked her if she too had heard these words, but she had not.

I truly believed that God had just performed a miracle to encourage my own heart that was hanging low while I was dragging my own feet, kicking up dust, dreading that I had done too little. In fact, I *had* done too little but was reminded that salvation does not depend on how well I share the message—everything depends on God and *his* power, *his* ability, *his* work. God was able to use me even in my weakness. God's truth was witnessed to this family living in the darkness of Islam. To God be the glory!

I am not sure what happened to Ting or her extended family. I know that Ting was under great pressure to find and marry an Islamic man and serve him in the home. I pray that even if her environment is not the greatest for studying God's Word, she will hold on to what she studied with her American friends and have further opportunities to share that truth with those walking in darkness.

# Letter From China

*Dear Kyle,*

*At one time, I almost lost my confidence of people's nature. I could not jump out of depression and sadness. I tried to search and explain everything, but failed.*

*You helped me to see it in a new angle, and suddenly everything changed. Since then, I adapted to now explain everything with the Bible. The more I knew the Bible, the more peaceful I felt in my heart. I began to solve problems one by one and build up the relationship between science and Christianity. After solving logical puzzles, I accepted my faith completely. One night, I suddenly felt that I need it just as I am hungry. I need food and water eagerly, and I am thirsty for faith to lead my life.*

*What's more, I was lucky to have a dear friend to help me and lead me to the right road. What impressed me a lot was the feeling after baptism. I could feel I was surrounded by something peaceful.*

*Later, I always felt happy and peaceful, no matter what kind of difficulties I met. I would not feel helpless. I know where my strength comes from. I can totally understand why you and other friends are so keen on your faith and would like to devote your lives to it.*

*Now there's only one regret in my heart—is it too late for me to know this? I lagged a long distance on my way, so I hope I will not waste my time to learn and grow. Dear friend, I hope we may know more with each other, and our God can lead us to get together. I would not like to waste my chance to know my brothers and sisters.*

*Sincerely,*

*Feng*

## Part Four

## The Seed

*. . . This is the passage of Scripture the eunuch was reading: "He was led like a sheep to the slaughter, and as a lamb before its shearer is silent, so he did not open his mouth. In his humiliation he was deprived of justice. Who can speak of his descendants? For his life was taken from the earth." The eunuch asked Philip, "Tell me, please, who is the prophet talking about, himself or someone else?" Then Philip began with that very passage of Scripture and told him the good news about Jesus. . . .*

# Food for Body and Soul

Learning Mandarin Chinese is incredibly difficult for many people, and my husband and I were no different. It was not easy for us to adjust to the concept that one syllable can mean four different things. For example, *ma* can mean "horse," "scold," "hemp," or "mother," depending on the tone. Despite the training we had received prior to moving to China, we knew desperately little Chinese when we arrived. We never intended to be able to speak about Jesus in Chinese. We hoped those opportunities would come with Chinese people who had been learning English.

We did need to know enough Chinese for basic survival skills, though, such as for shopping, taking a taxi, and eating out. However, even in those areas, our knowledge of the Chinese language was woefully inadequate.

In our area of China, very few of the "common" people knew any English, so our first few weeks of living in China were a huge challenge. We had a hard time figuring out how to prepare food. We couldn't even identify some foods in the marketplace and at restaurants. We were unable to go to a restaurant alone because we could not read the menu. But the Lord was well aware of our needs, and he had an answer in store.

We taught several English classes at night. Those who attended were either adults who worked during the day or students whose parents wanted them to get extra English lessons.

One night as we were walking home from class, we had almost reached our apartment when we heard footsteps running behind us and the voice of a woman calling to us. To our surprise, she was one of the best English speakers we had encountered so far. She told us that she loved learning English. She had wanted to become a teacher, but her family was too poor to send her to college. She worked as a waitress at a restaurant just down the street from our apartment. She told us her Chinese name and that she was 19 years old. She wanted us to give her an English name and to practice speaking English with us. We gave her an English name, and she called us "Aunt" and "Uncle," which is the polite way in China for younger people to address adults.

We invited her to come and see where we lived, and she invited us to eat at the restaurant. Our first meal there was quite humorous. She kept bringing in people for us to meet. So as not to overwhelm us, she brought them in one at a time. First her father, then the manager, then the manager's wife, followed by the cook and several of her friends.

Our friendship with this woman grew stronger from that point on, and in a mutually beneficial way. She fed our bodies by interpreting the menu at the restaurant for us, and we fed her soul by telling her about Jesus every opportunity we had. She had been brought up in a Muslim background. She had never seen or heard of the Bible or of Jesus. We told her things little by little, had her read for us bits out of our English Bible, and eventually gave her a Chinese Bible of her own. We invited her to our Christmas celebration. At Easter, we gave her a basket with candy and Christian literature. We taught her how to use e-mail in hopes that we could always keep in touch with her.

We saw her for the last time the day before we left China. I asked her if she had been reading the Bible we had given her. She said that she read it every night. I told her that Jesus loves her. She said that she knows Jesus loves everyone who believes in him. I told her that Jesus loves *everyone* in the whole world and that he died for *everyone* in the whole world and that those who believe in him as their Savior will be taken to heaven with him after they die. I encouraged her to keep reading her Bible and to introduce herself to the teachers that would be replacing us so that they could tell her more about the Bible. We planted seeds which we hoped others would water. We pray that the Holy Spirit works faith in her heart, and we hope to see her in heaven.

# A Bigger Plan

God is so good.

I was just sitting in the coffee shop sipping my *nǎi chá* ("milk tea") when I experienced a life-molding encounter. God humbled me, and then he picked me up with a loving grin and whispered, "Trust me."

I had just gotten done teaching advanced Bible courses. We had an amazing class exploring the Third Article and the Holy Spirit—our encouraging coach and gentle gardener. I had packed my laptop so that I could go straight to a coffee shop and work on our worship service for the next day's contemporary service. That was my plan, and I thought it would be a pretty effective one.

I got to the coffee shop, ordered myself a *nǎi chá*, and saw a perfect booth open upstairs. As I ascended the stairs heading for this booth, I suddenly realized that I had forgotten the power adaptor for my laptop back at home. So, to my regret, I left some books on the table to reserve it and asked a man in the choppiest of Chinese if he could watch my things until I returned in a few minutes.

I quickly boarded the subway, annoyed with myself for

ruining my perfect plan for the afternoon. By the time I got home I was extremely sweaty, so I changed into a T-shirt, got the adaptor, and hopped back on the subway to resume my now shattered plan.

I got to the coffee shop and went up the stairs again to find a young Chinese woman sitting in my booth! Frustrated, I took a deep breath. The woman was finishing some chocolate cake and saw that she had invaded my spot.

She apologized in near-flawless English and got up to go. "I'm so sorry. I'm almost done. I'll leave."

My mood softened. I replied, "No worries. Take your time. We can share. What's your name?"

"Carolyn."

"With a 'C' or 'K'?"

"With a 'C.'"

"My name is John."

"Nice to meet you."

"Nice to meet you too. What do you do?"

"I'm a housewife."

"Cool. I'm an English teacher."

"Nice."

"How is your English so good?"

"I've been studying by myself for three years. Also I'm married to a Chinese Canadian who worked in Canada for 17 years."

"Wow! That's a long time."

"I'm sorry that I took your spot."

"No problem. I was teaching some friends about Jesus and wanted to do some work here after, but I forgot my adaptor for my laptop. So I left my books here and went back home and then came back."

"You teach a class about Jesus?"

"Yeah. It's awesome!"

"To Americans, right?"

"No, to Chinese friends."

"Wow! I have always wanted to learn about the Bible but never met anyone who cared to teach me."

"This is so amazing! I'm leading a Bible study tonight at my apartment! I would love for you to come."

"I'll be there!"

"There are no accidents with God. Wow! I'm so glad I forgot my plug. Let me get your phone number."

"Okay!"

"So do you spell your name with a 'C' or 'K'?"

After Carolyn left, I started to cry. God's plans are so much higher than mine. Our Abba's mission is to fill heaven, and he will use anything to save the lost . . . even my own forgetfulness.

# The Sower and the Seed

In our city, the teachers before us had participated in Bible studies with friends, but nothing formal had been organized. However, there was an English class being offered by another teacher next door to our apartment as a way to build relationships. We decided to help with the class to get to know people. After a couple of weeks, we wanted to see if it would be possible to start a Bible study. At the end of one of the English classes, we announced that everyone was invited to come to our apartment the following Saturday evening to study the Bible and learn about Jesus. We had no idea how many people might come.

The night of our first Bible study arrived, and our Chinese friends started showing up. The pile of shoes outside of our door grew until we realized that *every single person* who had been attending the English class had accepted our invitation to study the Bible! What an amazing blessing!

Knowing that many of them most likely had not yet seen a Bible or heard about Jesus, we started the study by talking about the parable of the sower and the seed to show what happens when people hear and believe God's Word.

As we went through the lesson, our friends asked questions and discussed their thoughts. They said they didn't want to be the seed that was planted in rocky places and scorched by the sun as soon as it sprang up or the seed that grew only to be choked by thorns. God was with us in his Word that night, planting seeds of faith in the hearts of our new Chinese friends.

A few weeks later, we went with some of our friends to observe a registered Three-Self church service. It was a huge church with thousands of members, and as we sat up in the balcony, our friends helped translate the basic message of the service.

Afterward, two of our friends who had been attending our Bible study for just a few weeks observed, "All they talked about was how to be a good person and what we are supposed to do. They never mentioned what Jesus did for us!"

What a blessing it was to hear that statement of faith from them. God was working in their hearts, and they were already starting to identify teachings that weren't found in Scripture!

We had fairly regular attendance at our weekly Bible studies for the rest of the year, and the English class also continued as a way to make new friends and open doors. When we left China after a year of teaching, a pastor from our synod was called to water the growing seeds God had planted in our city. Eight years later, the Chinese people in this location are still served by a pastor and even more teachers—providing multiple opportunities for Bible studies and fellowship. It is truly amazing to see the power of his Word in China.

# Eternal Friendships

My first contact from your organization were Luke and Abby at the age of seven, when I had attend my first Bible study with them. Even though I was already a Christian before meeting them, the memories of that day have not faded.

> *Jesus loves me, this I know,*
> *For the Bible tells me so.*
> *Little ones to him belong;*
> *They are weak, but he is strong.*

When I walked into my friend Hong's house, this is the song that I heard. With accompany of two foreigners, Hong and some other little girls were singing hymns to glorify God. After they saw me, the foreigners welcomed me and asked me to join them. Having the heart of a little girl, I felt shy and embarrassed among the foreigners. But to my surprise, the hospitality of the foreigners soon made me feel comfortable.

After the class was over, I found myself enjoying my first Bible study with the two foreigners.

On the way home, my mom asked me if I want to come again.

My answer is definite. "Why wouldn't I come again?"

After I attended few more Bible studies in Hong's house, it was moved to my house. Because of the time I spent with them, I began to learn more about the foreigners. I learned that the foreigners, Luke and Abby, were Americans and had come to China to spread the gospel.

Every Thursday, Luke and Abby came to my house joyfully to teach other little girls and me Bible stories.

With a little girl sitting on Luke's lap and others sitting around Abby, our Bible study always began. First, Abby will pull out some colorful papers with song verses and pictures on it. After we had chosen which song we want to sing, the room was filled with the pleasant singings of little girls.

After we had used our voice to praise God, the next step is to read a Bible story. Using the way of going around the table, each of us will read a sentence, either in English or Chinese. Sometimes we read the story of Jesus and his disciples; sometimes we read the psalms of David; and sometimes we read the experience of Jonah inside the whale's tummy. Every time when the story we read was adventuresome, God's solving of the problem in the end always makes us want to praise him.

After we finished reading our story, the time left is for entertainment. In most of the times, drawing and playing card games is our way of ending the study.

In each Bible study with Luke and Abby, the other little girls and I learned more about Jesus, as well as his amazing grace for us. As time pass by, Luke and Abby did not only become my friends, but also became my brother and sister in Christ.

One Thursday, Luke and Abby came to my house with some heavy bags. After they unpacked, we saw what they brought were some beautifully decorated gifts. As Abby and Luke hand us a gift, every little girl's eyes were shiny. After I slowly got rid of the cover of the gift, a totally new Bible revealed itself to me. I really appreciated Luke and Abby for giving me a present. As I turned the pages of and carefully observed it, I find out that the New Testament of this Bible is in red and had two bookmarks sticking inside.

Soon after getting the new Bible, a Christmas party was held. And not long after the Christmas party, a news from Luke and Abby made me feel both excited and grieve: Luke and Abby would be going back to America to be married! I felt exciting and happy for their marriage, but in the same time, I am sad to be apart from them.

After saying good-bye to Luke and Abby, we little girls began to have Bible study with other teachers. Even though these teachers were sweet and tender, I still missed Luke and Abby. Because of this, I often send e-mails to them with the help of my mom.

Soon after Luke and Abby left China, I began to be homeschooled. In my years of homeschooling, God's guidance was always with me. He led me through my hardships and blessed me with his mercy and grace.

Similarly, Luke and Abby also received blessings from God. Within three years of living in America, they had become parents of two cute little boys.

One day, when I finished a long day of work and wanted nothing but relax, my mom told me something that made me come back to life again. She said that Luke and Abby were coming back to China!

Few months later, they came to my house for dinner along with their sons Henry and Jack. I constantly look out the window to see if they are coming. After a hundred times of watching out the window, the moment I had been waiting for arrived.

The car stopped right in front of my house, and people came out. Here they are, Luke and Abby, with Henry and Jack, in my house again!

During the dinner, my parents asked Luke about the Christian elementary school he is teaching at in Beijing. After Luke had explained about the school, my parents decided to send me there.*

After two years in that school with Luke as my main teacher, I became a ninth grader. As I grow and study to become a mature Christian, the experiences with Luke and Abby when I was little will be in my mind forever. I will remember this is not only because of our long-lasting friendship, but also because of the love from God they had for me and the seed they had planted in my heart.

---

*The elementary school is a private, Christian school founded and operated by teachers from our mission organization. Several years ago a few parents approached our teachers and asked for full-time Christian training for their children. Today more than one hundred kids are enrolled from prekindergarten through 9th grade, with another 40 families on the waiting list. The school is not officially registered with the government due to the religious nature of its work, so parents who enroll their children are effectively removing their children from the Chinese education system—a decision they do not make lightly. The school has moved locations several times due to security concerns. Nevertheless, God continues to bless and prosper the ministry.*

# Plant and Pray

Across the street from my apartment was a small hole-in-the-wall restaurant with excellent (and cheap) Chinese food. I would often stop in for lunch on my way to and from work. The owner, Lin, lived in the back of the restaurant with his wife, her parents, his grandmother, and his two young children.

Whenever I walked into his restaurant for some dumplings or noodles, Lin would greet me with a huge grin, and I would shake his hand and smile. He knew very little English, and I knew even less Chinese, but somehow we always managed to have a "conversation," and our friendship focused a lot around giving each other gifts whenever we saw each other. He would give me fruit to take home, and I would bring his children candy and toys.

One day he noticed the cross necklace I was wearing and asked if I was a Christian. After several minutes of using a smart phone translator, we worked out that he had heard some things about Jesus and wanted to learn more. Through a piece of jade jewelry and a smart phone, God moved our relationship from one focused around sharing physical food to sharing spiritual food!

The next time I visited, I brought him a Chinese/English Bible, and each time after that I brought study materials and bilingual books to help Lin study the Bible. While we ate together, we would talk about God, the gospel, and Baptism, and I could see the Holy Spirit working on his heart.

One day I came to his restaurant and Lin had a very sad look on his face. He told me quietly, so that his mother- and father-in-law couldn't hear, that all of the books I had given him were gone! He was certain that his grandmother had taken them and thrown them out. It was then that I learned how difficult it was for Lin to become a Christian and why his grandmother never quite warmed up to me visiting the restaurant so often.

"Despite this, I am determined to keep studying the Bible," Lin said through a translator.

It's hard for me to imagine how great a struggle that was for Lin. As a pastor's kid having grown up in America, I have never had to worry about offending or alienating myself from my family to become a Christian. This is a struggle that so many of our Chinese brothers and sisters do have to face.

I'd like to say that I learned the ending to Lin's story, but God had other plans. Summer arrived, and I went back to the United States to visit before returning to China. When I got back in August and visited Lin's restaurant, he was gone! The new owners said he had moved back to his hometown in another part of China. My prayer now is that the seed God planted in Lin will continue to grow.

As Christians, God tells us to go and make disciples. We don't always see how God uses us to share the gospel, but we know that he does. We don't often see the full picture from beginning to end, but God does. God may use one person to plant, another to water and nurture, and another to encourage, correct, or teach. The constant through all of it is that God is in control and the Holy Spirit is working. The important thing for us to do is to *go*. What an exciting and humbling joy it is for all of us to be a part of God's plan!

# Letter From China

*Dear friend,*

*I am very excited to communicate with my brothers and sisters on the other side of the earth. I still remember clearly the first time that I talked with my Christian friends. At first, I just felt unbelievable that there were really people who believed in Bible. In the past 20 years I had never meet a real Christian. I respected my new dear Christian friends that I met, and I just stored my understanding of that book.*

*I believe all happened since that day. There was a seed in my heart. Little by little, it grew. I waited for long. Every week, I took the class and learned as much as I could. Even if I was busy, there was a strength to drive me to continue. There were a lot of good teachers who tried hard to help me grow. Then I built up the general knowledge of Bible and Christianity. Now I have a faith that is growing stronger with Bible. Thank you for helping me grow.*

*Your friend,*

*Xiu Ying*

## Part Five

## The Washing

*. . . As they traveled along the road, they came to some water and the eunuch said, "Look, here is water. What can stand in the way of my being baptized?" And he gave orders to stop the chariot. Then both Philip and the eunuch went down into the water and Philip baptized him. . . .*

# English Corner

A friend and I were on our way to our first English Corner at a local university. We asked each other, "What if no one will talk to us? What if we end up standing there all alone?"

"They will come," replied a young Chinese man who was walking next to us.

English Corners are sessions held regularly at Chinese schools that are meant to help Chinese students practice their English. Usually the students talk to each other, but once in a while native English speakers visit to help the students with their oral English.

We knew this would be a good opportunity to meet some native students, so we decided to go to see what would happen. The students definitely came!

While we were still a few yards away from the wooded, outside area, we were spotted—two foreign girls who were willing to be drilled with questions for the next two hours. We didn't know what to expect, but we didn't expect what happened. As soon as we arrived, people flooded around us to talk. My friend and I were separated quite quickly, and we both had anywhere from 10 to 20 students surrounding us at one time. It was overwhelming and exhilarating at the same time. We talked about our favorite foods, the reasons we moved to China, and what our jobs were. We described the places we had already traveled to, and we told them where we wanted to visit next.

I met hundreds of people at English Corner throughout the years. I added numerous phone numbers to my phone and answered countless questions. Most of the conversations were shallow, but once in a while I met a special person who dared to go a bit deeper. Those were the ones that made English Corner special. A few were touched by our conversation in more ways than just spoken English practice.

One time I was in a conversation with a young man who had recently studied abroad and was trying to find a job that paid enough money. He was pressured to live up to the high expectations of his family regarding his career, even as a recent graduate. I talked about my job, my humble salary, and my vast amount of student loans. He was shocked to hear that I didn't seem worried.

"I don't have to be worried about money," I replied. "God is in control. I'm careful with my money, and I know he will take care of me."

We continued to talk about the comfort and peace I have knowing Jesus is my Savior and that this world is only temporary. I planted a seed—I shared the reason for the hope that I have. Now I pray that others continue to water that seed in his heart and that that Holy Spirit will make it grow.

During another visit to English Corner, I met a girl who would someday become my sister. As usual, there was a large group of Chinese students around me. People came and went after they asked all of their normal questions, and I repeated my answers over and over. However, there was one girl who remained at my side. No matter where I went or who came and left, she was right there, listening intently to what I said and occasionally asking questions. Honestly, I was a little annoyed that she just wouldn't leave me alone.

By the end of English Corner that day, though, something in me said that she was a girl whose number I should get so I could meet with her again in the future. So, we exchanged numbers and went our separate ways.

I sent her a message the next day, and we decided to meet for lunch. After the food arrived, I asked if I could begin our meal with a prayer. She respectfully said yes, and I thanked God for giving us the opportunity to meet and asked him to bless our time together.

As we lifted our heads, she immediately responded, "Are you a Christian?"

"Yeah, I am. Are you a Christian?" I asked.

"No, but I studied with some foreigners in my hometown during my undergraduate studies."

*Wow, is it that easy?* I thought to myself. "Oh, I do Bible studies in my apartment too—want to join?" I asked.

She faithfully attended studies for the next two years. After many different conversations about the Bible and Christianity, I could tell she still had reservations about what she was learning. However, one day we were talking about Baptism and the blessing it is to be a child of God. I asked her if she wanted to be baptized. She was surprised— she didn't think she could be a Christian. She thought there were special requirements. It was an awesome day when I had the opportunity to tell her that God doesn't require anything to be his child. He loves us as we are.

One month later we finished studying what the Bible says about Baptism, and she told me she was ready to be baptized. I had the privilege of watching my friend and sister in faith go from doubts and questions to belief and faith.

English Corners are intense. There are a lot of people who want to talk with native English speakers. But while English Corners can be exhausting and disheartening, they can also be used to serve God's plan. To this day, every time I attend this simple event I pray that God will use me to reach a lost soul. Perhaps I will only be a light, maybe I will only plant a seed, but possibly I will walk with a new friend in his or her life of faith. Thank God for English Corners.

# The True Perfect

My experience in China began with two years in a mountainous city in Zhejiang province. It is a lovely city, but tough for new teachers since there is no university and few people there speak English. From the beginning, I knew that our organization was planning to leave the city unless I decided to stay a second year. While we had a few strong friendships, there were just so many other cities that needed to be reached. I wrestled with the decision about whether to return or not, but eventually decided to return to that city for a second year. I was sent one new teacher to work with. The beginning of the school year was rough. Shifting from five teachers to two meant plenty of additional teaching hours for both of us. Yet God had a plan and a purpose for our second (and final) year in that city in Zhejiang province.

One day during that second year, one of my local Christian friends introduced me to my colleague, Shu. According to my friend, Shu was interested in Christianity, so I searched for opportunities to get to know her. Shu was quick to explain that she had attended a house church a few times while she was in graduate school. She had enjoyed learning about the Bible because of its historical significance. However, the house church leader tried to force her to be baptized after she had attended three or four times. She never went back.

The failed baptism had happened three years earlier, and Shu's life was very different at the time that I met her.

"My life is perfect right now," she told me.

She had recently moved to Zhejiang province to be closer to her boyfriend. They had been dating about two years, but he had been pursuing her for seven years prior to that until she finally said yes to a date. Shu had a well-paying job that she loved and plenty of colleagues who had already become close friends. Shu was bright, friendly, and a natural leader.

Since Shu's current life really did seem "perfect," and since she was still distant from the church, my conversations with Shu started with discussions of the afterlife and, soon after, about sin. We spoke over lunch in the school cafeteria about sin and God's grace, and I encouraged her to start reading the gospel of John. One evening while I was out with my friends, Shu called me and confessed faith over the phone. The Spirit worked faith in her heart just two weeks after we started talking!

Shu then started attending our team's Bible studies and was so excited to learn more about her new friend Jesus. She invited many of her friends to our studies and was working through a full introductory Bible class in preparation for her baptism. Her life had completely changed, but she was struggling with one lingering problem. Her relationship with her boyfriend, Xiaofei, was not going well. He completely rejected her new faith life and said he would become a Buddhist monk if she became a baptized Christian.

Soon after, they broke up, and Shu was baptized. Fortunately, Xiaofei didn't become a monk, and the two of them continued to keep in touch. One day, Shu told Xiaofei he shouldn't be so opposed to something he knew so little about. Xiaofei thought that was a very good point, so he decided to attend our Bible studies as well.

When Xiaofei initially joined our studies, he was only trying to find flaws in biblical logic. His attitude affected the environment of our studies. We readily admitted we didn't have all the answers, but we answered as many of his questions as we could. He kept joining our studies and gradually asked fewer and fewer questions. Shu prayed for him every morning and evening and kept praying daily while she was on a trip over the summer. Then one wonderful day she received an e-mail from him saying he was thankful he had found a Savior in Jesus Christ!

The news was true! The Spirit had worked in Xiaofei through the Word during conversations with another Christian teacher over the summer. By the grace of God, Xiaofei was washed by the Holy Spirit through Baptism!

Our organization stopped sending teachers to that city after that summer. Thanks be to God, immediately after

Xiaofei was baptized, he stepped up to be one of the three local leaders of their own small house church.

Shortly after, I traveled down from Shanghai to be the best man at Xiaofei and Shu's Christian wedding service. Ten months later, I received a phone call when their daughter, Liling, was born. She was baptized a month later! What started out as a Sacrament that caused doubt in Shu's mind became the miraculous means to saving faith for her and her family! It is amazing to know that Liling has Christian parents who are teaching her God's promises from infancy on.

Looking back, it is easy to see how God worked through us in our final year in that city and that God was guiding me in my decision to stay a second year. He had a plan for Shu, for Xiaofei, and for their little daughter. The small group of believers still meets for weekly Bible studies to encourage one another in God's Word, and both Xiaofei and Shu also continue to use their unique skills and gifts to bless their house church.

# Overcoming Obstacles

One decision that every Chinese adult has to make is whether or not they would like to be a member of the Communist Party of China (CPC). The CPC guarantees its members a better job with high status, good working hours, and good pay. Also, some promotions are reserved only for Party members, so if they are not a member, they may risk plateauing on the corporate ladder.

To join the Party, Chinese adults must go through a multifaceted process. They must be voted in by their classmates (if they are a student) or their colleagues. They also need to take a class to learn about Communism and how the Party benefits the Chinese people, and they need to pass a test at the end of the class. They need to write reports about the Party and apply for membership, and if they are accepted and decide to become a member, they need to vow that they will be loyal to the Party and not be a part of any religious fellowship. Therefore, Party members cannot be Christians.

Fei was a sophomore in college. He wasn't the smartest student in his class, but he worked hard and gained the respect of his classmates and professors. He was class president and spoke at various class events. He also studied the Bible with us. He was friends with many Christian Americans and actively took part in activities and studies. He was living his dream of being a student and enjoying life.

After studying God's Word with us for eight months, he realized that Jesus was his Savior and the only way to heaven. He desired baptism. We were excited and planned his baptism date. However, earlier in that week, he was presented with a challenging question. His teacher had asked if he wanted to be a part of the Communist Party. Getting in would have been easy. He had the respect of his classmates and recommendation of his teacher. It was a difficult choice: choose the Party and have the comfort of knowing he could have a good job with a secure future or choose God and be guaranteed difficulties in this world but have confidence that he can eagerly await the next.

Thanks be to God, Fei chose baptism. He chose to put his life in God's hands and trust that he would be okay. He picked the path with difficulties now and peace eternally. He became a redeemed child of God and a brother in Christ.

Now, Fei is still following the path of eternal life. His faith goes up and down, just as all Christians experience, but he knows that no matter where he is and what he is doing, he has the promise of God remaining by his side and supporting him along the way.

Not all Chinese people would choose this path. There is

an extra dose of faith needed to give up life as a Party member and live life as a Christian. Pressure from society and family would cause most students and employees to choose the safe path, deny religion, and become an atheistic Communist. Some parents do not allow their children to be baptized because it could negatively affect their chances at receiving a good job in the future. These are the people we have the privilege to work with. God uses us to show them that only he has the power to transform their lives in ways the Party never could.

# Can You Help Me?

"Alice! Come outside!" my roommate called. "We have chicks!"

*Chicks?* Indeed, as I hurried outside, I found chicks running in our little backyard—the "bike lot," as we called it, because it was the only safe place for everyone's bike. Two fluffy, yellow chicks had wandered over from our neighbor's yard. Our neighbor's mother-in-law came outside carrying a box with more bobbing fluffy heads. We all smiled and laughed as we handed back the two babies.

A few days later the sun was shining, and I was sitting on the stairs in the bike lot reading my Bible.

Our neighbor peaked her head out the door and asked in English, "Did I hear you singing worship songs?"

I needed to make a quick decision, so I prayed, *What do I say, Lord? Is it safe to witness? Help.*

I then answered, almost immediately, "Yes."

"Oh, I am so thankful to hear. I have been looking for somewhere to worship, and I haven't found one yet. Can you help me?" she asked quietly.

"Yes. I would love to!" I replied.

She told me her name, and I shared mine. We set up a time to get together and study God's Word.

I later learned that she had spent time in Russia and was multilingual. While she was there, she met a friend who shared the gospel message with her, and she was then baptized. Since she had returned home to China, she had not found a church home.

We became her new church home. She and I met a few times each week and read through a portion of the Bible. As we dug into God's Word, she often said to me, "I never understood what it meant. This is so wonderful!"

Every time she left our studies, I would thank God for her. I don't know who felt more strengthened in her faith, she or I? What an amazing blessing to share God's love and grace.

One day, after we finished studying, she said, "Tell me again about Baptism."

I discussed with her God's Word and the water in Baptism. We talked about becoming a child of God.

She replied, "Should I have my daughter be baptized? What if she grows up and gets mad at me for having her baptized? What if she becomes left out because she was baptized and none of her friends were? What if something bad happens to her because she is baptized?"

Her questions caused me to mentally freeze. I had never had to face such thoughts in America. I had never imagined the fears a Chinese Christian parent faces. What comfort did I have to give her? I reminded her of God's promises. "So do not fear, for I am with you" (Isaiah 41:10). "And surely I am with you always, to the very end of the age" (Matthew 28:20). "And we know that in all things God works for the good of those who love him" (Romans 8:28).

She said she would call me as soon as she and her husband decided, and she left my apartment. Soon after our door closed, I heard her door close. One minute passed, then two . . . and then my phone rang.

"How about Friday night?" she asked.

That Friday night we met at my apartment with another teacher and a bowl of water. Her husband was present as well. He too believed in Jesus but chose not to be baptized as he was a member of the Communist Party and fearful of the possible outcomes. With his daughter and wife he was all smiles.

Another teacher baptized their daughter. She had a smile that covered her face while the water was sprinkled on her and the words of God were spoken.

My friend and I hugged and shed tears together, and her husband looked so very proud and happy for his daughter, who at that moment became a child of God.

My friend turned to me and said, "I know God will take care of her, no matter what happens."

That very Sunday my friend and her daughter both joined us to worship. We sang songs of praise and said prayers for her and her family. She never missed our worship time together while I was there. She always made time to learn more about God and his love for her and all people.

When I left China, it tore at my heart to say good-bye to her. However, that was not the end of the story. In the following year, my friend asked another teacher to visit her family who lived in a different part of China where other Christian teachers lived. The teachers that lived there were able to go to her family's home and share the amazing message of God's grace with them also. A few years after that, she called me from the United States and said that her daughter was attending a Christian preschool.

God's plan be praised!

# Letter From China

*Hello Jennie!*

*Happy Christmas. I am going to be baptized on Sunday! I am so excited. I am hoping to be one of Christian family members. I will be soon! You are all my sisters and brothers. Thanks God gave me many lovely sisters and brothers and sent you and all friends around me to help me get close to God. And God let us study his words together which help me a lot to understand his words.*

*How lucky I am. God loves me so much. It was God who rescued me from the hell. Last year my life was totally disorder. I felt lonely, fear, helpless, and hopeless. Nobody could comfort me. I didn't want to live any longer. Not until an "angel" sent by God took me close to God and helped me understand God's words, my life become brighter and brighter. I feel like I was reborn. The old Jing has gone, and I am the new Jing. Thanks God and thanks all of you.*

*Sincerely,*

*Jing*

# Part Six

# The Proclamation

*. . . When they came up out of the water, the Spirit of the Lord suddenly took Philip away, and the eunuch did not see him again, but went on his way rejoicing. Philip, however, appeared at Azotus and traveled about, preaching the gospel in all the towns until he reached Caesarea.*

# Mr. So-So

"Excuse me, where are you from?"

I was headed back to my apartment, minutes before a Bible study. Having already lived in China for over a year, I was used to this conversation. It was common for a college student or an educated person to approach me wanting to practice English. I thought this was no different.

I squinted in the shadows of the night, trying to see who it was. A man quickly appeared, wild hair spun in all directions. As he approached me, he asked the same question again. His hand, grimy from the day's work, met mine in a sudden handshake.

I thought of making a hasty escape. After all, I had friends arriving at my apartment at any minute. I answered his question, and as he rambled on in a mix of broken English and Chinese, I found strange joy in his eyes. How could this man who worked an apparently long shift be filled with such happiness?

The conversation turned into him attempting to sing a song by the Backstreet Boys—loudly—and then I knew I had to invite him to our study. I needed to get to know more about this charismatic man.

As we walked to my apartment, I learned that he had never graduated high school but studied English from his old textbook. He was actually a farmer from a small village several hours away and came to the city as a migrant construction worker. At the time, millions of migrant workers, considered to be uneducated people with little wealth, came to the city to work on various construction projects. This man was no different.

Before the class began, I told him that we would be studying the Bible. I wasn't able to tell him much about the Bible because he was so interested in meeting everyone there. I realized then that his ability to understand English was quite limited. Though we read the Bible in both English and Chinese, I wondered how much this man actually understood. Near the end of the study, the leader asked a question to which this man perfectly proclaimed the saving gospel message. Everyone was stunned at his bold confession.

He told us that he had been a Christian for some time, having been taught the gospel message by Chinese missionaries who had visited his farming village many years ago. After that night, he came to several more Bible studies. His enthusiasm for sharing God's saving love was contagious, and his passion became an inspiration to everyone who met him. Wanting to share this message, he gave himself an

English nickname—"Mr. So-So"—which he explained meant "God saves and uses oneself to save others."

Not long after I met Mr. So-So, he disappeared just as quickly as he came. Many might look at a man like Mr. So-So as someone who has very little in life. Yet Mr. So-So didn't think so.

# Echoes of Praise

We wanted Easter to be a special celebration, so we found some white flowers in the market and planned some special music for the Bible study that day. As our Chinese friends took off their shoes at the door and settled on the couch, chairs, and floor, there was an air of excitement. We shared the amazing story of the resurrection and ended with the hymn "I Know That My Redeemer Lives."

One of our friends, Shen, seemed to have really caught the feeling of celebration. As he left the Bible study, he loudly sang over and over, "I know that my Redeemer lives!"—just that line. It echoed through the cement stairwell and probably raised a few eyebrows, but it sounded like pure joy! Wouldn't it be amazing if Christians around the world spontaneously sang praises as they left church?

# Will Not Return Empty

Li Hua is constantly seeking out opportunities to grow in her faith, including coming to multiple studies a week and setting an example for me by making time to read her Bible regularly. She cherishes fellowship with Christian brothers and sisters. At the same time, God also uses her as a light for her unbelieving coworkers.

She took a short trip to Thailand with these coworkers. The trip was full of sunshine and exotic food, but she also brought back one disheartening experience that stood out to her. While walking outside at a market, her group walked past a beggar. Her friends started discussing the beggar's deformities and what could have caused them. Moved to use this as an opportunity to witness, Li Hua bravely chimed in, speaking about how all are beautiful in God's eyes and how he created everyone with a plan and purpose.

Li Hua was immediately shot down. Her coworkers denied that any such love could be possible. Retelling the experience to me later, she shared, ". . . and in that moment, I doubted God's words." Although she is strong, she confessed that sometimes even as she witnesses she finds herself doubting or struggling to stand firm when she is standing alone.

But she doesn't give up.

Sometimes God makes witnessing opportunities incredibly obvious and even irresistible to us. This past year, Li Hua was handed one of these opportunities. Li Hua's company—a training center for students preparing to study abroad—asked Li Hua to create and teach a Bible course for students pursuing an education at private schools that required religious courses.

When describing the expectations for the course, the company told Li Hua that her job was to teach, but not to make her students Christians. Clearly the company didn't know that God's Word does not return empty but achieves the purpose for which he sent it. As she planned the courses, Li Hua asked me for materials and videos to help engage her students. I gave her what she needed and was even able to give a copy of a Chinese/English Bible to each student. Li Hua knows that she may never see the outcome of these lessons on the hearts and minds of her students, but how awesome that God used her to plant the seed!

The community of Christians God is growing here is an awesome reminder to Li Hua that she is not alone as she continues to mature in her faith. Our prayers are that she never feels alone and that she stays encouraged and bold in sharing the Good News with all.

# A Light in the Darkness

A look into the life of my friend Rou beautifully illustrates the importance of looking to heaven as our eternal home while we often feel like strangers here in this world.

Rou is unique among most of our Chinese friends in that she grew up regularly attending church with her family in her hometown. When she got to college, God led her to take an English class that was taught by a Christian teacher who invited Rou to come to a women's Bible study that I also attend.

For the past several months, Rou has come to every women's study that her busy schedule allows. She shows her servant heart by coming early to help prepare dinner for everyone and by translating Christian songs for our study.

I have never seen her grades, but I would imagine that Rou is acing every one of her courses. She is talented, ambitious, and diligent in all aspects of her life, including her faith life. A while ago, she told me that she wished to read the whole Bible but was not sure where to start. It was awesome to help her develop a plan to grow closer to God.

Almost all of Rou's friends and even her boyfriend are

not Christians. She has shared how frustrating it is that others—especially those so near and dear to her—just don't get why her faith matters so much to her. She feels like a stranger. However, she knows this isn't her eternal home, so with the help of God, she lives a life of service to him.

Several months ago, Rou invited her close friend Zixi to attend women's study with her. Watching Zixi experience the fellowship of Christian sisters and grow to know her Savior has been a joy. But what makes it even more special is knowing that Rou was the one who invited her to come.

One thing that challenges me personally about my work here in China is that I feel like I will never be able to do enough! There is just so much work to do and so many opportunities to be a light, and I always feel like I should be doing more. For example, I host Bible studies in my apartment, and my living room should comfortably seat about seven people. However, we gather on stools and perch on couch armrests with as many as 18 Chinese friends each Bible study. Filling my apartment with friends is always bittersweet because as much as I love those that are in attendance, I can't help but think about the millions of people all over the city that are not hearing the saving message.

The point is that while I came here to share Jesus with China, China doesn't fit in my apartment. Eighteen people barely fit in my apartment. But the good news is that God is not just working through me. He is also working in the hearts and souls of every friend who comes to a study. Like Rou, those friends go home to their families, friends, classmates, coworkers, roommates, boyfriends, and spouses. They are lights to the unbelieving world.

All Christians are strangers here on earth. May God continue to bless our ministry work here in China as we look forward to the day when we will be strangers no more.

# Western Culture Class

One of the first people I met when I moved to China was a lady by the name of Wei. A few months after I arrived, Wei was baptized as a child of God. She boldly told everyone she met that she now considered this day her birthday! The seed of faith was first planted in Wei's heart in the late 1980s by Canadian students she went to university with. She appreciated learning about the Christian religion, but at that time in her life she saw no need for any religion. For more than 20 years, that small seed was inside of her, but nothing happened to it. Finally, one of her closest friends invited Wei to one of our Bible studies. Going to that study changed her life forever. Ever since, she has been going to many studies and continues to grow in her faith. It may have taken more than 20 years, but that small seed is now a strong tree of faith.

As a child of God, Wei wants all people to come to know their Savior the same way she knows him. She has preached God's Word to her family, her friends, and even her colleagues at work. Wei is an English teacher at one of the most prestigious schools in her province. Most of her students receive full-ride scholarships to top-ranked universities in Europe and the United States.

One day, during my time in China, Wei decided that she also wanted to share her faith with her students. She came to our group and asked if some of us could teach a Bible class at her high school. I was shocked! I wondered how it would be possible for American Christians to enter a Chinese public high school and teach the Word of God. In America, where we have the freedom of religion, Bible classes are generally not allowed in public schools, so I didn't understand how this could be allowed in a country that is officially atheistic. But Wei told us it would be okay and that God would guide us.

So I, along with another teacher from our group, began teaching a one-hour class once a week on the Bible. Because of generous donations from Christians in the states, we were able to give each of the 30 students a Chinese/English Bible. We started with basic stories, such as Moses, David and Goliath, the Christmas story, and a few parables. It was a joy to see the excitement on my students' faces as they learned about a God who loves them. By the end of the semester, a few kids even said they wanted to be Christians! God's Word was actually being taught in a Chinese school to Chinese students!

When we returned from our almost two-month break for Chinese New Year, we were ready to resume the Bible class at the high school. However, Wei called and said the class had been canceled. The superintendent of all the high schools in the city found out what Wei was doing and told her to stop immediately.

I was heartbroken, but also scared for Wei. She could potentially lose her job or even get arrested. As an American, the worst likely punishment for me would be getting kicked out of China. But Wei could be in so much greater trouble. However, despite all my concern, Wei once again told us not to worry. Together we said a prayer of thanks that we had those few short months to share the Good News with her students.

The next day, I received another phone call from Wei. She said the class was back on! I was so confused. Wei explained that her coworkers saw what a blessing the class was for the school, even though most of them were not Christian, and they wanted her to continue having the class. So instead of calling it a Bible or religion class, this class was now classified as a Western Culture class. As long as we taught more than just the Bible, the class could continue. Throughout the whole semester, we taught 11 Bible classes and one class on American poetry. That way, we could rightfully say we taught more than just the Bible. It is all by God's grace that everything worked out smoothly.

On the first day of the second semester, as the new students filed into the classroom, we noticed that seven of them were returning students from the previous semester. They told us they loved our class and opted out of another elective in order to take our class again. Here were seven students going to one of the best schools in the province who chose to give up a grade in another class to audit our class. To them, hearing more about the Bible was more important than getting another good grade.

A few tears rolled down my cheeks as I began teaching that day. It was so amazing to see the hand of the Holy Spirit in that room.

Sadly, after that second semester, the school did not allow us to teach there anymore. Yet for one year, two American teachers and a strong Chinese Christian woman shared the Good News to a group of high school students. While none of them were able to be baptized at that time, I pray that the seed that was planted takes root. I pray then that the root grows, and, even if it takes 20 years, I pray that those students someday share the Good News with those around them, just like Wei did. To God be the glory!

# An Unlikely Meeting

Sometime in November of 2013 I met Qiang, the pastor of a small house church in Ningxia, who is now, by God's grace, also taking pastoral training courses through our organization. We met for dinner in a small house—his house—and had a marvelous "you-can't-get-more-authentic-Chinese-food-than-this" kind of dinner. It's a miracle that it happened. In fact, it shouldn't have happened. There were far too many roadblocks in the way. Here's the story:

The first thing that I had to overcome was my complacency. I grew up in a tiny rural town in the Midwest. I was rooted there, and I was totally happy in that environment. I had no visions of life in another country, not even thoughts of traveling very far. My world was no larger than a 500-mile circle. I didn't feel a need for change.

My attitude was another barrier that got in the way of meeting Qiang, or anyone for that matter. When my wife and I arrived in the small Chinese town we would call home, God's work seemed hopeless to me. While our colleagues in China's large cities were finding many opportunities to teach about God, I struggled to see the point of any kind of work in our town. Even if I did tell someone about God, there was no confessional church in town to encourage them to attend so they could continue to get good spiritual food. There was only the local Three-Self church, and it took no stand on things like Baptism and the Lord's Supper. In addition, I felt that even if students were open to coming to Bible classes in our home, they would someday leave town, and we would have no resources to give them when they went off to other cities. So, my attitude and heart were not optimistic.

There was another reason that it was unlikely that Qiang and I would meet each other. Qiang's father had been a Chinese government official. That means that Qiang had to become a member of the Party. Being a member of the Party requires that the person denounce Christianity and adhere to atheism. So Qiang's father, mother, and he were atheists. Little chance that he and I would find each other in this world or the next.

But Qiang's father died in 1995. At that time, Qiang, his mother, and his wife became Christians. For a while they attended the local registered church, but comparing what was taught there and what was taught in the Bible, they saw a discrepancy and left. They attended a house church for a while, and when their pastor left, Qiang took over as pastor.

Qiang's ministry was only a small part of his life, though. He already had a full-time job. His trade was what in the States we would call pipe fitting. He maintained the hot water radiator heating system at a local hospital. The city had a few boiler plants that supplied hot water to most residences. They decided when to turn the heat on in the fall and when to turn it off in the spring. Qiang's job required that he also be a certified electrician.

So, God was at work. He had guided me to move to the town where Qiang lived, and he had moved Qiang and his family to faith through the message about God's love in the Bible. However, there was still a barrier to our getting together. I spoke no Chinese. Qiang spoke no English. Little chance that we would connect. So close and yet so far apart.

Then Akuan came into the picture. Akuan was a 26-year-old graduate with a degree in business administration. He grew up in Guangzhou, formerly known to us as Canton, in southern China. A handsome man and a man of the world, Akuan was an atheist. But Akuan found that his beliefs left him empty at times, and he would withdraw and brood over his emptiness and become deeply depressed. Some college friends asked him to go to a small house church with them, and this was his first contact with God of the Bible. As a modern student, Akuan also had to learn English and spoke it quite well. And while his mother tongue was Cantonese, he also spoke Mandarin "with a heavy Cantonese accent," according to him. At that point, Akuan was thousands of miles from being in the town that I lived in.

Akuan had always wanted to help other people, so he volunteered for charitable work through the government for a two-year commitment. They offered him a small stipend and sent him to work in the coal mines that we lived near. While looking for a church in our town, Akuan attended the registered church. There he met some Chinese friends of my colleague and was soon invited to weekly lunch gatherings at my colleague's apartment. I also attended those gatherings, so I met Akuan. Later Akuan found Qiang's house church and stopped going to the registered church, but he still continued to meet Sunday afternoons with my colleague and his new friends.

One day Akuan came to my apartment to talk. He told me the deeply moving story of his spiritual life. We listened and talked. A few days later, Akuan told me that his pastor (Qiang) wanted to meet me and have me preach and teach at his church. In the end we agreed to first meet for dinner at Qiang's house, and Akuan said he would be our interpreter.

So there I found myself, eating a "you-can't-get-more-authentic-Chinese-food-than-this" kind of dinner, served by Qiang and his wife. Finally God had brought together the country boy from small-town America and the Chinese government official's son in a house in a small Chinese town with an interpreter to help them. I asked lots of questions and heard his story, but I wasn't sure what he wanted from me. Then I remembered something I had learned in my training. It has been observed that house church pastors often have no formal training. So in the lull of conversation, I asked Qiang if he had gotten any training. He paused for a while, and a strange look came over his face. Then he spoke loudly in Chinese to Akuan. After a while, Akuan explained: Qiang had been praying for months that God would send him someone to give him the training he needed to be able to function as a pastor! I was stunned. I told him that I would be happy to help him however I could and that I knew my colleagues had course materials that could give him what he had been praying for. He explained that they had left the registered church because of its emphasis on living a good life and its lack of the preaching of sin and grace. I told him how we teach our pastors to preach Christ, sin, and grace in every sermon, no matter what their text.

When I left in the taxi that night, I was on an emotional high. My wife was excited with me about what had happened. I immediately e-mailed our organization's program director to inform him of what had transpired.

Our mission agency has the perfect materials and courses for pastoral training, and Michael was the pastor in China who was in charge of administering these courses. He just so happened to be planning a trip from his home in Beijing to a city an hour south of our town three days from then. Michael was immediately notified, and he quickly arranged to stop in our town. We all worked fast to make the arrangements. Michael stayed with us, and he took the time to explain the pastoral training program to me, giving me materials for organizing and teaching the subjects that some call pre-seminary preparation.

How did all of this happen with such perfect timing? I, of course, knew this was all part of God's great plan.

I couldn't sleep that night that I met Qiang. By many standards, our meeting shouldn't have happened. I had put too much trust in what I can see and little trust in what God can accomplish on his own. God knew what Qiang was longing for and needed, and he knew how he had prepared me through training and many experiences for that exact moment.

I'm happy to say that my wife and I still live in this small town, and we have become weekly guests for dinner at Qiang's home. Qiang and his wife never make the same meal twice. Always very delicious food, and plenty of it. Afterward we study the Bible for three hours.

So even though we had planned a "generous" one-year gift of time out of our lives to come to China, we'd really like to finish the pastoral training course with Qiang before we leave. That probably means we will be here for three years. God willing and our health permitting, we will.

# From Pupil to Preacher

It was Bible study night. A friend of a friend brought some other friends hoping to practice their English and obtain some American culture. They were all young college students and all working toward their master's degrees in some type of material sciences. We offered our usual smorgasbord of hot water, tea, and cookies made American-style with plenty of butter, sugar, and chocolate chips. Broken English swirled around the room as introductions were made and study started.

Jian says that he came to that first study to meet a girl that he liked. He says that he was impressed by how gracious and kind we were to him. He also says that he *loved* the cookies. For those reasons he came back again the next week. And again. And again. And again. Thirty-nine more times.

Things didn't work out with the girl. I ran out of chocolate chips. But Jian kept coming back to hear about the one thing he really needed. He didn't miss a study that entire year. This young man with fractured English and a goofy smile became a fixture among the dozen or so Chinese that studied God's Word with us. As his knowledge grew, so did the depth of his questions and answers. Every so often, without warning, he would cut in and translate concepts that were difficult for others to understand.

A year went by, and we watched Jian grow. We listened when Jian told us he was spending too much time playing video games. We sympathized when he lamented over not finding a girlfriend—a pressing matter second only to finding a job for most Chinese people ages 25 to 30. We prayed when Jian told us he wasn't sure what he believed about the Bible. When we left China to return to America, we cried.

It was hard to say good-bye to it all—the mission work, the language, the travel, the food, the dear friends, and even the standing-room-only buses. As with all of our Chinese friends, we prayed for Jian's faith and anxiously awaited updates. Jian did update (fractured English and all), and the news he shared was good:

"Every day I pray and read three chapter of Bible. . . . When I listen to some songs about Jesus, my heart can be calm. . . . I can feel the changes in my life. Praise to Jesus! . . . I will get baptism on this Thursday. I think it will be a good idea. I will remember this day as my rebirth day all my life. I hope you can share the joy with me. . . . I feel my understanding about Bible grow more and more, and I can help more people. . . . I still enjoy the pastor course last year and passed all the exams. This year I have the idea to serve God in your team. . . . I just consider to take the seminary course next year and quit my job."

Three years after my departure from China, I had an opportunity to return for a visit. For a whirlwind two weeks I was able to embrace old friends, encourage their faith, eat delicious food, and stand on crowded buses. Included on the itinerary was a Sunday morning service led by pastor-in-training, goofy-grinned, cookie-loving Jian! Nothing could have prepared me for the overpowering emotions stirred in my heart that morning.

There he stood—the student, now teaching. The young man once sitting at our feet being fed from the Word, now feeding me the Lord's Supper. And as I stood in front of him, head bowed, hand out, listening to the words "Take and eat" spoken in Chinese, I was overwhelmed by God's grace. By his perfect will. By the *incredible* power of his Spirit transcending every language barrier, yet promising the same salvation using the same simple Word. (What power there is in that Word!)

With tears streaming down my face, my shoulders shaking as I tried to compose myself, I silently took my seat and praised God's holy name. Who was the teacher? Who was the student? During our time together and our years apart, we had both been sitting at the feet of our Savior, all because God chose to use one girl, one plate of cookies, and the miracle of God's Word.

# Letter From China

*Hi Michael!*

*Thanks again for your job, and this is great encouragement for me. I was baptized in this June and soon I know I was born surely for God. The time God prepared for China is coming, which excites me all the time.*

*Thank you and thanks many people who are working for Chinese. I believe that one day every student at my university will have the chance to hear the evangelism, and this is my dream! To spread evangelism!*

*Thanks and hope God bless you forever.*

*For the glory of our Father,*

*Min*

*Dear Lord, the Almighty and my Redeemer,*
*Let our desires have no greater joy*
*than to hear more people walking in your truth.*
*Let our hearts be bound to your Great Commission.*
*Let your will be our will until the end.*
*We know that we are far from what you demand,*
*and we are asking far more than what we can be,*
*but we know you are able.*
*Come Lord, guard our hearts and minds*
*so that we can follow you. Amen.*

—**J. Li, seminary student**